THE BATTLE OF ITTER CASTLE '1945

STEPHEN WYNN

Pen & Sword
MILITARY

AN IMPRINT OF PEN & SWORD BOOKS LTD.
YORKSHIRE - PHILADELPHIA

First published in Great Britain in 2024 by
Pen & Sword Military
An imprint of
Pen & Sword Books Ltd
Yorkshire - Philadelphia

ISBN 978 1 39900 707 8

A CIP catalogue record for this book is available from the British Library.

Typeset in INDIA by IMPEC eSolutions
Printed and bound in England by CPI (UK) Ltd.

Pen & Sword Books Limited incorporates the imprints of Archaeology, Atlas,
Aviation, Battleground, Digital, Discovery, Family History, Fiction, History, Local,
Local History, Maritime, Military, Military Classics, Politics, Select, Transport,
True Crime, After the Battle, Air World, Claymore Press, Frontline Publishing,
Leo Cooper, Remember When, Seaforth Publishing, The Praetorian Press,
Wharncliffe Books, Wharncliffe Local History, Wharncliffe Transport,
Wharncliffe True Crime and White Owl.

For a complete list of Pen & Sword titles please contact

PEN & SWORD BOOKS LIMITED
George House, Units 12 & 13, Beevor Street,
Off Pontefract Road, Barnsley, S71 1HN, UK
E-mail: enquiries@pen-and-sword.co.uk
Website: www.pen-and-sword.co.uk

or

PEN AND SWORD BOOKS
1950 Lawrence Rd, Havertown, PA 19083, USA
E-mail: uspen-and-sword@casematepublishers.com
Website: www.penandswordbooks.com

THE BATTLE OF ITTER CASTLE '1945

Contents

Introduction

Had it not been for the Second World War, the thirteenth-century Itter Castle, situated as it is some 2,000 feet above the entrance to the Brixental Valley in the Tyrol region of Austria, would have had no real place in modern history other than being a picturesque building whose history could be traced back to Roman times, when its location formed part of the main travel route between Italy and most of the rest of Europe. The village of Itter can be found some 10 miles west of the popular Austrian ski resort of Kitzbuhel. The first castle built at Itter was completed in 1240, but after being destroyed, was later rebuilt in about 1530.

The Brixental Valley is more than 18 miles in length and for a period of 500 years between 1312 and 1805 was part of the state of Salzburg, when it came under the rule of the newly established Kingdom of Bavaria, before finally becoming part of the state of Tyrol in 1816. By this time the castle was already in a ruinous state, having been inexcusably allowed to reach such a condition by the Bavarian government.

Over the years the castle has had many owners, including the famous nineteenth-century Emperor of

France Napoleon Bonaparte. Because of its remote location, many of its owners rarely lived there, and over time it became nothing more than a ruin; an eye sore and a blot on the landscape.

The castle in its present form was built on the foundations of its predecessor after it was purchased by a German businessman, Paul Spiess, in the nineteenth century. His plan was to turn the new building into a high-end hotel. Work on returning the castle to its former glory began in 1878, and was completed six years later in 1884, although its hoped-for success as a hotel never materialised. Instead, Spiess decided to cut his losses and sell the building to the German composer and pianist Sophie Menter, who made it her home for the next twenty years. Thanks to her ownership of the castle, some of the world's most renowned musical greats of the era are known to have stayed there, including such composers as Franz List and Pyotr Ilyich Tchaikovsky, as well as Arthur Rubenstein, the Polish-American pianist who many still regard as one of the greatest pianists of all time, and who was such a prestigious talent that he first performed with the Berlin Philharmonic Orchestra in 1900 when he was just 13 years of age.

Menter sold the castle in 1902 after the cost of its upkeep had become unsustainable. The new owner was the German businessman Eugen Mayr, who carried out further renovations and improvements, including electric lighting and running water, before turning it into the Schloss Hotel Itter. Despite its success as a hotel, it was sold to the deputy governor of the Tyrol region, Dr Franz Gruner, who primarily used it as a holiday home.

The castle was first leased by the German government in 1940. Officially it became the headquarters for the *Deutscher Bund zur Bekämpfung der Tabakgefahren* (German Association for Combating the Dangers of Tobacco). Hitler disliked the habit of smoking with a passion, to such a degree that he forbade anybody from smoking in his presence.

By the latter months of 1942, Itter Castle was being openly used as a detention centre by the SS for what they called, *Ehrenhäftlinge* (honour prisoners). On 7 February 1943 it was seized on the orders of Heinrich Himmler and turned into a prison specifically to hold prominent, mainly French, individuals who were deemed to have some bargaining value in case Nazi Germany found itself in a position of having to agree peace terms with the Allies. To this end, it officially became a subcamp of the notorious Dachau concentration camp.

The Tyrol region of Austria had been left largely untouched by the ravages of the Second World War. The area, with its high mountains and remoteness, provided the Nazis with a natural refuge for the enormous amounts of ill-gotten money, gold, artworks and religious artifacts they had pilfered from banks, art galleries, private dwellings and individuals from numerous countries throughout Europe. Indeed, it is believed that the Nazis dumped somewhere in the region of £4.5 billion of gold, platinum, and jewellery into Lake Toplitz, an isolated lake that can be found in the very heart of a dense forest in the Alps.

The area was finally liberated by American forces, mostly from the 88th Infantry Division, during the first week of May 1945. On 9 May, Germany signed a document of unconditional surrender with the Allies. It was during this time that the Americans started to discover the hiding places the Nazis had used to conceal the large numbers of stolen artifacts.

Everything was set up for the Nazi forces to fight to the death against the advancing Allies, as they dug into defensive positions throughout the Alps. Allied commanders had believed that these die-hard forces of the SS would deploy what was known as 'Werwolf' tactics, involving the use of a guerilla resistance-type forces who would operate behind enemy lines, creating mayhem, panic and uncertainty. This tactic would be used hand in hand with other German forces, who would operate as a defensive front line.

It was feared that the Germans might use the region, along with other Nazi-owned territories, to make a last-ditch stronghold in the Alps and fight to the bitter end. However, this did not occur – mainly due to the announcement of Hitler's death in his Berlin bunker. This in turn led to chaos amongst the dwindling Nazis ranks, who knew that the war was nearly over and that they were not going to be on the winning side.

The Battle of Itter Castle in May 1945 was without doubt one of the most unusual events of the war, being one of only two known occasions when Allied and German forces joined together and fought alongside each other. Whether that was out of basic humility or an understanding that with the war rapidly drawing to a close, the victors would be looking to capture and punish those who had been responsible for carrying out any wartime atrocities, is unknown. Either way, it happened, and regular American and German soldiers joined forces to fight against a unit of SS troops hell-bent on re-capturing the castle and its primarily French captives who were being held there. What their fate might have been had they been captured by the SS remains unclear, but it would have more than likely changed the history of France and been yet another blight on the German nation for years to come. After all, those held in the castle included some of France's most experienced political and military minds, some of whom would go on to shape French politics in the post-war years, including two former Prime Ministers of France, Édouard Daladier and Paul Reynaud, along with the sister of the leader of the nation's Free French Forces, General Charles de Gaulle, Marie-Agnes Cailliau.

CHAPTER ONE

The Beginning of the End

The exact date of the beginning of the end for Nazi Germany is debateable, but one worthy of consideration is D-Day: Tuesday, 6 June 1944, the beginning of the Allied landings in Normandy in northern France, when the full invasion of German-occupied Europe began.

On this day more than 150,000 American, British, Canadian, and French troops landed over a 50-mile stretch of the French coast as they took part in Operation *Overlord*, the largest seaborne invasion history has ever seen, along with nearly 200,000 naval personnel as well as 10,000 airmen.

Initially the invasion did not look to be going the way the Allies had intended it to, as the first day objectives of linking all five landing beachheads, as well as capturing the towns of Carentan, Saint-Lô, and Bayeux, were not achieved. Caen, which was a major objective, was not captured until 21 July.

The main problem for Nazi Germany was that despite knowing an Allied invasion of Europe was imminent, they did not know exactly where it was going to take place, which meant they could not concentrate their defensive forces at any one location. Instead, they were spread out along the entire length of the Atlantic Wall, which stretched from the northern-most tip of Norway all the way down to the border of France with Spain.

Germany's best chance of preventing Allied forces from making their way inland and gaining any kind of foothold was to prevent them from coming ashore in any significant numbers. If the Allies were defeated on the beaches and forced to retreat to their landing craft and back across the English Channel to England, the war could have dragged on for years and possibly not resulted in an eventual Allied victory and the end of Nazi Germany.

On 18 June, less than two weeks after D-Day, the worst storms to hit the Normandy area in more than forty years struck, resulting in the loss of more than 800 Allied vessels, along with damage to large sections of the temporary Mulberry harbours, which had made the required capture of the port at Cherbourg even more important.

When the Allies drew up their plans for the Normandy landings, they knew they would need to secure a deep-water port, such as the one at Cherbourg, to allow much-needed reinforcements and equipment to be brought directly from the United States. The fighting to capture the port at Cherbourg continued until 29 June, when German forces guarding the harbour, as well as those inside the main garrison, surrendered, but not before the German defenders had so badly damaged the port of

Cherbourg, and mined its waters, that the port was not fully usable until the middle of August, although the first ships were able to arrive in late July.

Within two months Allied forces had gained a stronger foothold in Europe; they had defeated the German Army in France, with the Allies reaching and liberating Paris on 25 August. Large crowds of French civilians lined the Champs Elysees to watch the Allies make their way into Paris. It is interesting to note just how quickly, and easily, German forces had 'capitulated' with the loss of somewhere in the region of 200,000 casualties, killed or wounded, with the same number of men having been captured.

The Allies did not stop once France had been liberated. Instead, they continued the fight, forcing the Germans to continue their retreat all the way back to the very heart of Germany. By April 1945 the war was all but over. The Allies were at the 'gates of Berlin': the Americans, British, and French from the west, with Soviet forces making their way from the east. The race was on, and it was simply a case of who would get to Berlin first. As for the city's civilian population, it was a case of the lesser of two evils. After the aggression, brutality and lack of compassion German forces had shown towards the Soviet population during their invasion of 'Mother Russia' as part of Operation *Barbarossa*, the thought of what might happen if Soviet forces won the race was almost unthinkable. The truth of the matter, however, was that there was little to be gained either strategically or militarily by taking Berlin, and any such victory was purely for propaganda purposes.

By April 1945, the US 6th Army Group had reached Austria and became involved in the fight to dislodge and force the surrender of all German forces in the area in the first week of May.

Elements of the US 3rd Infantry Division were the first Allied troops to arrive at Berchtesgaden, which they captured, with the remnants of German Army Group G surrendering to US forces at Haar, in Bavaria, on 5 May. The local residents of Berchtesgaden had become used to seeing top members of the Nazi Party frequent the area; it was where Adolf Hitler had a holiday home, known as the Berghof, located in the Obersalzberg region of the Bavarian Alps nearby. At about the same time the US 103rd Infantry Division had made its way through Bavaria and into Innsbruck, Austria, where they would see action at the Battle of Itter Castle.

A number of well-known French prisoners had been held at the castle since before the war, with the intention of using them as bargaining chips with the Allies. These included politicians, including former prime ministers, senior army officers, a tennis star and the sister of the leader of the Free French Forces, General Charles de Gaulle. There were real concerns by the prisoners that elements of the SS known to be in the area would attack the castle with a view to killing those being held there. To prevent any such attack from taking place, American and Wehrmacht soldiers joined forces to defend the French prisoners, as well as the castle, from the fanatical SS forces.

Despite it being blatantly clear by the time of the Battle of Itter Castle that the war was rapidly coming to end, and that the Allies were going to be the victors, several German units surprisingly still chose to continue the fight. For those Nazis deployed throughout southern Germany and Austria, they at least had the safety net of knowing the Soviet threat towards them was somewhat reduced because of the latter's focus on capturing Berlin.

Returning for a moment to the point about German forces, including those men of the 17th SS Panzergrenadier Division 'Götz von Berlichingen', who took part in the attack on Itter Castle, the obvious question must be why? When the Nazis came to power in 1933, military personnel had to take a new oath. Prior to this time such 'oaths' had always been taken to protect the nation and uphold its constitution, but the new oath was changed so that those taking it, which included members of the SS, swore an allegiance to Adolf Hitler. This having been said, the question has to be asked, why, after Hitler's reported death, did all military personnel simply not surrender, as surely once he was dead, any oath of allegiance sworn to him became null and void? One possible explanation as to why SS units continued to fight after hearing of Hitler's demise was because a number of the men who served in SS units were not actually German, but foreign recruits. This, coupled with the fact that many of them feared they would be shown no quarter if they surrendered or were captured, saw no other option but to continue the fight until they were killed in action, which, as far as they were concerned, at least guaranteed their deaths would be honourable ones.

Maybe it was naivety, maybe it was arrogance, maybe it was a bit of both, but after Hitler's reported suicide, his successor, Admiral Karl Dönitz took it upon himself to set up a new provisional German government in the northern city of Flensburg, situated as it was close to the border with Denmark. Dönitz even believed he was in a position to be able to negotiate with the Allies to gain favourable terms in a subsequent peace agreement. It was also possible that he was just being hopeful, maybe even delusional, as it did not appear to have even crossed his mind that the Allies, acting in a collective sense, would accept nothing less than Germany's absolute and unconditional surrender of all her military forces.

CHAPTER TWO

Itter Castle

At the outbreak of the Second World War, Itter Castle was owned by Dr Franz Gruner, who had purchased the property in 1925 when he was the deputy governor of the Tyrol region. Due to the castle's extreme remoteness, however, it was not somewhere he spent much in.

Despite having been in Austria since the Anschluss in March 1938, the German government only leased the castle from Gruner in 1940. The use of the word 'leased' is interesting, because it suggests that Gruner had a choice in the matter. Maybe he did, but fearing the possible consequences if he failed to acquiesce to their demands, it is also possible that he simply went along with the arrangement for his own safety, or maybe what he was being paid by the SS under the terms of their agreement was sufficient to make him not care? Whatever the truth of the matter is, it is unclear as to whether he knew the real purpose for what the Nazis wanted to use the castle for.

During the Second World War the requisitioning of large private dwellings was common practice on both sides. On such occasions the Wehrmacht were known to have paid the owners a fair price for the inconvenience caused. The SS, on the other hand, were not so concerned about following the agreed conditions of German military policy if they did not feel inclined to do so. Instead, they simply took what they wanted, especially if they felt there was no need to foster healthy relationships with the local population.

Dr Gruner died on 23 January 1941, at the relatively young age of 45, and was buried at the Ottakring cemetery in Vienna. His passing was both sudden and unexpected, but there is no suggestion that Himmler or the SS were in anyway responsible for his death.

Heinrich Himmler ordered that Itter Castle should be seized on 7 February 1943, two years after Gruner's death. Afterall, why continue paying for it when they could simply seize it at no cost? The only real surprise is why they simply did not seize earlier.

It is interesting to note that the castle was transformed into a prison to house high-profile detainees more than two years before the end of the war. Is this an indication that Nazi Germany doubted they would win the war as far back as 1943?

The man tasked with carrying out Himmler's instructions for the castle was SS Obergruppenführer (Lieutenant General) Oswald Ludwig Pohl, who besides being the head administrator of all Nazi concentration camps, was also in charge of the SS Main Economic and Administrative Office. After the war, Pohl initially managed to evade capture, but was eventually arrested in May 1946, having been discovered hiding out near Munich whilst working as a lowly farmhand. Pohl's trial, which began at Nuremberg on 8 April 1947 and concluded on 3 November 1947, was the fourth of thirteen war crimes trials which took place in the German city. Pohl was found guilty and sentenced to death by hanging. There then followed a number of appeals on Pohl's behalf against his conviction and sentence, before it was finally upheld on 11 August 1948. Despite this, he was still not executed until 7 June 1951 when he went to the gallows at Landsberg prison.

An officer from Dachau concentration camp, SS-Hauptsturmführer Sebastian Wimmer, was put in overall charge of the changes made to the castle. Fortunately for him, several prisoners who were detained at the main camp had worked as tradesman before their incarceration, and it was at Itter Castle that their particular skills were put to good use. Despite its intended purpose, many of the castle's contents such as furniture, paintings, books, and silverware were crated up and sent to another location for safe keeping.

Just over ten weeks after the castle had been initially leased, it was fully transformed from a stately residence into a prison, but not just any old prison. There were no cold, steel doors or basic conditions as would have been the case for the common soldier, or those held for political reasons at regular POW camps. The accommodation at the castle was now more akin to that of a five-star hotel, even though all the nineteen bedrooms were intended for double occupancy. Part of the conversion also included accommodation for the German guards who were to be stationed at the castle. The only one of them to have been allocated their own room, which would have included ensuite facilities, would have been the German officer in overall charge of the castle, Sebastian Wimmer.

The sole purpose in requisitioning the castle was for the specific detention of certain individuals who had been designated as *Ehrenhäftlinge* (honour prisoners), who were detained and held in relative comfort, as was in keeping with their potential importance to Nazi Germany. Hitler had the misguided belief that the prisoners could later be used to gain more favourable terms in any future surrender negotiations with the Allies.

Despite its actual purpose, the castle was officially referred to by the Nazis as an *Evakuierungslager*, or evacuation camp, and was put under the operational control of the Dachau concentration camp, which was situated about 90 miles away to the north and included some 197 other satellite camps that were dotted throughout northern Austria and southern Germany.

During the early stages of their incarceration at the castle, life for the VIP prisoners, it would be fair to say, was extremely good. Besides receiving three 'square meals' a day, which they were free to eat wherever they wanted to within the castle's walls, they were also provided with alcohol, most of which was in the form of fine wine, as well a financial allowance. Life at the castle was certainly very different to a 'normal' prisoner of war camp or one of the Nazi's concentration camps. Indeed, the difference between Itter Castle and these other camps is difficult to comprehend.

The one similarity which could be drawn between Itter Castle and the camp at nearby Dachau, for example, was that both were patrolled by armed guards who were there to ensure that none of the inmates escaped. Anybody at either camp ran the risk of being shot if they even attempted to escape; a scenario that everybody understood.

By 1944, the hardships of war had even started to be felt at Itter. Food and fuel were becoming increasingly more difficult to source, which resulted in what could only be described as deprivation for both prisoners and guards alike. Accepted norms such as the use of electricity throughout the castle became an unobtainable luxury, and during the hours of darkness, candles were used.

Those held within the castle were intelligent individuals, although it would not have required a genius to have worked out that such shortages at a prestigious location like Itter Castle was a direct reflection of the state of the war from a German perspective. There were those amongst the prisoners who interpreted this to mean that the war would be over sooner rather than later, but they were also concerned about their personal safety and worried what the Nazi hierarchy would do with them if they felt the war was lost and that they were no longer of any value.

In many respects the decision to use Itter Castle as a prison was an obvious one, as it was already a substantial structure which did not really require much in the way of additional work to ensure that those being held there would find it extremely difficult to escape from. With many of the castle's bedrooms simply being designated as 'cells', the addition of a few extra locks, armed guards, floodlights, and copious amounts of barbed wire covering the tops of the castle's high walls, made its conversion complete.

The man put in charge of the castle's new inhabitants was SS-Hauptsturmführer (Captain) Sebastian Wimmer, of the 3rd SS Panzer Division 'Totenkopf'. Born in Dingolfing, Germany in 1902, Wimmer joined the Munich police in March 1923, a couple of months after his twenty-first birthday. Having reached the rank of sergeant major, he was dismissed from the force in February 1935 for unknown reasons, but within just a couple of weeks had enlisted as an officer in the SS and found himself stationed at the newly opened Dachau concentration camp.

Just after the outbreak of the Second World War, Wimmer was serving with the newly formed 'Totenkopf' Division, the majority of which was made up of concentration camp guards from the SS-Totenkopfverbände (SS-TV, or 'Death's Head' Formation), as German forces made their way into Poland and participated in the murders of Polish civilians, both political and non-political, as well as Polish POWs.

Between January and September 1942, he had served with the infamous 2nd SS Panzer Division 'Das Reich', who on 10 June 1944, just four days after the Allied landings at Normandy, murdered 642 civilians in the French village of Oradour-sur-Glane.

In September 1942, Wimmer transferred back to the 'Totenkopf' Division, but this time found himself working at the Majdanek concentration and extermination camp, whose original use was a forced labour camp for foreign workers, including Russian POWs, Jews, and political prisoners of different nationalities. His role there was as the head of the protective custody camp, which in essence meant he was in overall charge of the running of the camp and was therefore complicit in the numerous atrocities carried out there. This included the use of firing squad executions, hangings, and the use of Zyklon-B in its gas chambers.

After only six months at Majdanek, in March 1943 he returned to Dachau as the deputy protective custody camp leader, where he remained until October the following year, before moving the short distance to Itter Castle to take charge of the captives being held there.

Wimmer's appointment as the Commandant at Itter Castle could certainly be described as somewhat unusual. Here was a man who had a reputation for displaying extreme brutality and cruelty in equal amounts to all those under his control. He did not even appear to care that much more about the lives and wellbeing of the men under his command. The obvious question is, why did the German authorities place a man such as Wimmer, with his reputation, in charge of some of their most celebrated wartime prisoners? From his perspective, living in the comparative luxury of a castle must have been more of an attractive proposition than living at Dachau concentration camp, and all the degradation associated with it.

There must have been a sound reason behind appointing a young man just 24 years of age to such a position, but the many decades that have since passed have made it harder to understand. It is difficult to believe that Nazi Germany could not have found an older, wiser, more experienced, and better suited officer for such an important position. Maybe it was because of his murderous capabilities and his blind devotion to 'the greater cause' of Adolf Hitler and the Nazi Party that he was put in charge? It was quite possible that a situation might arise when the Nazi regime, realising that they no longer had a need for such 'high value' prisoners, decided they would want them killed instead. If such a scenario ever became a reality, they would need somebody to carry out the killings without question. It is more than conceivable that senior Nazis believed Wimmer was that man.

To guard the castle's high-profile inmates, Wimmer was provided with a deputy, Otto Stefan, and just twenty-five guards from the SS-TV. The men of this unit were responsible for security within the Nazi concentration camp system across Europe. The cap badge of the SS-TV was the skull and crossbones, but to distinguish themselves from other SS units, they also wore the same badge on the right collars of their uniforms.

Historically, the members of the SS-TV tended to be older men whose only involvement in the war had been mainly as camp guards. This was a role they were more than happy to undertake, especially if it meant they did not have to participate in any actual fighting on the battlefields across Europe. Being posted to Itter Castle quite possibly saved the guards' lives, because when the main Dachau concentration camp was liberated by the 45th Infantry Division of the United States 7th Army on 29 April 1945, an unknown number of the camp guards there were killed by some of the inmates, as well as a number of the American soldiers liberating the camp, so shocked and disgusted were they at what they had discovered. Whether the SS-TV guards volunteered or were posted to Itter Castle to carry out their duties is unclear.

The guards' attitude towards those whom they were tasked with looking after at the castle varied quite considerably, with no one guard being the same as another. Human nature being what it is dictates that individuals will form different types of relationships with members of a group, depending on the individual personalities of each. The interactions between the guards and those they held captive at the castle were no doubt affected to some degree by the knowledge that the war was going badly for Germany and that they might well be on the losing side. The guards would have also been very mindful of how they interacted with the prisoners when their senior officers were about, knowing full well that if they appeared to be too over familiar with them, they could end up being posted to a frontline position, or one that was certainly more dangerous than the situation at Itter Castle.

One of the first of the VIP captives held at the castle was Albert Lebrun, who up until July 1940 had been the President of France before he was replaced by Philippe Pétain. For company, Lebrun had the former Italian Prime Minister Francesco Saverio Nitti, as well as the former French Ambassador to Italy and Germany, André François-Poncet. Their stay at the castle was only a brief one, and they had all left before the end of the war in May 1945.

Several prisoners from occupied Eastern European countries were also housed at the castle, but they were kept there purely for labour to help maintain and look after it. Two of these men, Zvonimir Čučković, a Croatian resistance fighter, and Andreas Krobot, a Czechoslovakian cook at the castle, went on to play important parts in the battle, as we will see later.

If an order to kill the prisoners was sent to Wimmer, it was highly unlikely he would have carried it out. Like the prisoners he now found himself in charge of, his focus was now on surviving the war. The last thing he needed was to be responsible for the murders of so many high-ranking individuals; an action he quite clearly could never escape the blame for. If anything, he needed to keep such individuals on his side to speak favourably about him at any post war trials he might become embroiled in. Although not the brightest of individuals in an academic sense, he was also not so stupid as to not recognise the potentially fatal predicament he would find himself in should Germany fail to win the war. His murderous and barbaric wartime actions would have undoubtedly seen him swing on the end of a hangman's noose in recompense.

Throughout April 1945, a number of high-ranking German officers and their subordinates, some accompanied by their families, arrived at the castle as they tried to escape from Soviet forces advancing from the east. They never stayed long as time was more precious than it had ever been. The castle provided a comfortable place to sleep and pick up a few provisions before moving on as they headed towards Germany and the advancing American and French forces, whichever came first.

The one man whose arrival at the castle on the evening of 30 April 1945, which no doubt alarmed those held there, was SS-Obersturmbannführer (Lieutenant Colonel) Wilhelm Eduard Weiter, who was also the last commandant of Dachau concentration camp. His reputation went before him, and word had reached those being held captive at the castle that he had been responsible for the murder of some 2,000 inmates at the camp not long before his departure. He was also believed to have been responsible for killing the German dissident Georg Elser on 9 April 1945. On 8 November 1939, Elser had attempted to assassinate Adolf Hitler by placing a bomb at the Bürgerbräukeller in Munich. The bomb exploded but did not kill Hitler as he had already left before the bomb went off, but it did kill eight other people and injured a further sixty-two. Weiter received a letter from Gestapo chief, Heinrich Müller, informing him that Elser was to be killed and that his death was to be blamed on an Allied air raid. The need for such an elaborate cover up is unclear, as is why Elser, who had attempted to kill Hitler, was not executed following his capture, but instead was held in captivity for more than five years.

Weiter was somewhat of an enigma. He had served in the German Imperial Army during the First World War, having initially enlisted in 1909, and went on to see action on the Balkan, Eastern and Western fronts, but ended the war as a regimental paymaster. Having left the army at the end of the war, he enlisted in the Bavarian police where he undertook a similar position as he had held in the army.

Weiter did not join the Nazi Party until 1937, having had no real political beliefs or interest in post-war Germany. It was enough for him just to have survived the war and be part of a new Germany, even though like many of his compatriots, he went through hard times as economically his once beloved country was at rock bottom. After joining the party, he came to the attention of SS-Obergruppenführer (Lieutenant General) Oswald Pohl, the head of the SS Main Economic and Administrative Office.

Following Weiter's arrival at Itter Castle, the obvious question in the minds of the French VIPs being held there was whether he had come to exact the same treatment out on them as he had to the prisoners at Dachau. Ultimately, they had nothing to worry about. Weiter did have death on his mind, but only his own. In the early hours of Wednesday, 2 May 1945, after an evening of heavy drinking, Weiter shot himself, an act which he certainly made hard work of.

Aiming for his heart, he missed, and finding himself still alive, he repositioned his weapon to the back of his head and pulled the trigger for a second time. On this occasion he was more successful in his endeavours and was killed immediately.

Weiter's suicide was somewhat intriguing, because despite his outward demeanour of displaying arrogance, violence and brutality in equal amounts, he was first and foremost a cowardly brute who once he realised the war was lost, simply took the easy way out, albeit with the aid of copious amounts of alcohol to help him on his way. He had probably guessed that once the war was over he would be called to answer for what he had done and had worked out that he would end up swinging on the end of a rope as punishment for his war crimes.

As the camp commandant at Dachau, he was not only the man in overall charge of its day-to-day running, but literarily held the power of life and death in his hands. He was more noticeable by his continued absence at the Dachau camp, preferring instead to delegate his minions to carry out what he deemed to be the more mundane and functionary aspects of the camp. He became so detached from his responsibilities that conditions for the inmates worsened dramatically as time went on, although this was not a situation which caused him much concern.

Weiter's suicide would appear to have played on the minds of Wimmer and his men to such an extent that they left the castle on or around 4 May, fearing the worst for their own personal safety at the hands of the enemy, particularly the Russians, if they stayed. The main consideration for them was what their fate would be if they sided with the Americans against their fellow Germans, albeit the SS, and then ended up on the losing side. Wimmer, who had the added concern of having his wife and young son with him, and his men decided not to hang about to find out.

An even more impressive and powerful looking 'castle' than the one at Itter was the thirteenth-century Kufstein Fortress, which at 1,663 feet above sea level quite literarily overlooked the town of the same name set out below it. This was also the next castle that Wimmer found himself in, although this time as a prisoner. The fact he was captured within a matter of weeks after leaving Itter Castle is not so surprising considering he was accompanied by his wife and young son, who would have certainly slowed him down and restricted how fast he was able to move.

What is really surprising is the fact that Wimmer was never charged with any war crimes at the end of the war, despite the fact he had been involved in mass murders in Poland during the early days of the war and had been head of the protective custody camp at Majdanek, and the deputy protective custody camp leader at Dachau, where thousands of innocents, mainly Jewish civilians, were murdered. How he escaped ever facing any charges relating to his wartime crimes beggars belief, and only the French authorities at the time could possibly provide the answer.

Wimmer was held in French custody until 1949, before being simply let go. There was no fanfare, no furore, nothing other than the release of just another man from prison in the post-war world, which even in that comparatively short period of time had changed so much. Indeed, it is staggering how a man such as Wimmer never stood trial for his crimes and was only held in captivity for a total of four years. There is no available explanation as to how and why he was dealt with so leniently.

He eventually returned to the town of his birth in May 1951 and moved back in with his father, without either his wife or son. It is known that he committed suicide the following year, but why he took his own life is unclear. Maybe it was because he had lost his family, or maybe it was to do with no longer having any power, no position of influence over others, a concept that he just could not cope with. During the war he was a 'somebody', a man with the power to determine if an individual lived or died. He was respected by his equals but feared by those under his control or command. Once the war was over, he became a nobody.

As for his deputy at Itter Castle, Otto Stefan, he became somewhat of a mystery over the subsequent years, as both his whereabouts and the date of his death are unknown. If he did survive the war, he was never captured by the Allies and was therefore never put on trial to answer any allegations against him for his wartime actions. It is quite possible that he simply changed his identity, dressed up as a private soldier and lost himself in their midst, greatly aided by the utter confusion which prevailed in the immediate aftermath of the war.

CHAPTER THREE

French Captives of Itter Castle

This chapter looks at the hostages who were held at Itter Castle, as well as a couple of German officers who ended up playing a prominent role in the events that took place there in May 1945. It also provides detail and insight into why the Germans would have deemed these individuals as potential bargaining chips in any future negotiations with the Allies.

Although held in what was quite possibly one of the nicest and most comfortable wartime prisons, the combination of characters held within the castle's walls was interesting to say the least, even though the atmosphere was certainly not as harmonious as one might have expected it to have been.

An aspect of their collective incarceration which the Germans had not considered, or if they had, then they did not really care about it, was that not all their French captives either liked each other or were even comfortable being in the same room as each other. It was a potentially explosive situation for them all to be in.

Some of these men had replaced each other politically or militarily, or had carried out the sacking of the other. A couple were active supporters of the Vichy regime, with one having even held a government position with them. Most of the others were supporters of the Free France movement, which was led throughout the war by General Charles de Gaul from his base in London.

To start with, Paul Reynaud and Édouard Daladier were not only former Prime Ministers of France, but they were political arch-rivals and enemies. Individually and collectively, they had absolutely no time for former supreme commander of the French armed forces, General Maxime Weygand, whatsoever. His crimes, as far as Reynaud and Daladier were concerned, could not be forgotten, or forgiven. Not only had Weygand surrendered to Nazi Germany in May 1940 in his position as the Supreme Commander of French Armed Forces, a role he took over from General Maurice Gamelin, but he had also initially collaborated with the occupying German forces. Having lost his position as Supreme Commander of French Armed Forces to Weygand, it would not come as a surprise for anybody to learn that Gamelin was far from being his biggest fan. Two others who did not exactly see eye to eye with one another because of their opposing political views were the Trade Union leader Léon Jouhaux and the anti-communist Colonel François de La Rocque.

For the entire time they were held at Itter Castle, the political rivalries and personal bitterness between the detainees remained in place. Although they were all prisoners, the groups did their best to avoid each other, even down to eating their meals at separate tables. On the surface it certainly did not appear to be a recipe for convivial conversation and a long-term co-existence, but with no other option in sight, the best had to be made of a bad job.

Those held captive at the castle included several of the great and the good of French society:

Jean Laurent Robert Borotra

Borotra was a famous French tennis player who was a dominant factor in world tennis during the late 1920s and early 1930s. He was also the Physical Culture Minister in Pétain's Vichy government between August 1940 and April 1942 and was arrested by the Gestapo in November 1942. He was initially detained at Buchenwald concentration camp near Weimar, in Germany before being transferred to Itter Castle, where he remained for the rest of the war.

His part in the subsequent fighting at Itter Castle was significant, as it was he who made it safely out of the castle during the fighting to try to locate Allied forces in the immediate vicinity and return with them to the castle.

Borotra was born in the south-western French city of Biarritz on 13 August 1898, and during his early school years it became obvious that intellectually he was an extremely bright individual.

It may have been that some of his steely determination to succeed was derived from the death of his father. Being the eldest of four children, he suddenly found himself as the man of the household at the tender age of 9. His early thoughts were not of becoming a famous tennis player, instead it was engineering which stimulated him and what he saw as his future career.

In 1912, to help improve his English, he was given the opportunity to live with a family in England for two months during the summer holidays. It was during this time that he was first introduced to the game of tennis.

By the outbreak of the First World War, Borotra was not quite 16 years of age, and was still too young to serve his country in its hour of need. As soon as he reached his eighteenth birthday, he enlisted in the French Army and was assigned to an artillery unit. He saw out the remainder of the war without being wounded or injured, which was somewhat remarkable as most of his time was spent in the French front lines, never that far away from danger and the possibility of a sudden and immediate death.

Borotra's military service did not finish with the end of the fighting. Instead, he remained in the French Army until the latter weeks of 1919. It was during this time where sport played a large part in French military life, and Borotra discovered he had a natural sporting ability, especially when it came to playing tennis. On completing his military commitments in the French

Army, he returned home to his mother and siblings in Biarritz. There he would spend many an hour honing his skills and practising different tennis strokes at his local tennis club with one of his brothers.

Despite his newfound love of tennis, Borotra returned to his studies, earning himself a degree in engineering at the acclaimed *Ecole Polytechnique* situated on the outskirts of Paris. Having qualified as an engineer, he found himself in somewhat of a quandary as the Grand Slams of tennis were only open to amateur players, a status which remained in place until as recently as 1968. Travelling all over the world to play in the major tournaments, especially the Grand Slams, cost money, which quite often meant that less affluent players, regardless of how good they were, could not always afford to take part in tournaments outside of their own country unless they had the independent financial means to do so.

Borotra won his first major tournament in Paris in 1924, in a career that would see him go on to win a number of further such events. This included his second French Open in 1931, the Australian Open in 1928, and Wimbledon in 1924 and 1926. In 1925, he was the runner up in both the French national championship and Wimbledon. His only appearance in the US national championship in 1926 saw him come off second best to his fellow French man, René Lacoste. He was the runner up in France for a second time in 1929, meaning that both of his French defeats were also at the hands of René Lacoste. He was also the runner up at Wimbledon in 1927 and 1929, with both defeats coming at the hands of fellow French man, Henri Cochet.

Borotra fared better in doubles championships, where he won nine titles in twelve appearances. He won the French Championship in 1925, 1928, 1929, 1934, and 1936. His victories in 1925 and 1929 were with René Lacoste, while in 1928 and 1934 he won alongside Jacques Brugnon. In 1936 he won his fifth and last French doubles title as the partner of Marcel Bernard. Borotra also won Wimbledon in 1925 with René Lacoste, and again in 1932, 1933, with Jaques Brugnon, with whom he also won the 1928 Australian Championship. His three losses came in the French Championship of 1927, with René Lacoste, Wimbledon in 1934, with Jacques Brugnon, and the 1939 French Championship, also with Jacques Brugnon.

Between 1925 and 1934, he also appeared in five mixed doubles championships, winning them all. In doing so he won all four Major tennis championships, each of the victories coming with a different partner.

1925: Wimbledon. Partner, Suzanne Lenglen (France).

1926: United States Championship. Partner, Elizabeth Ryan (United States).

1927: French Championship. Partner, Marguerite Broquedis (France).

1928: Australian Championship. Partner, Daphne Akhurst (Australia).

1934: French Championship. Partner, Colette Rosambert (France).

Along with his French counterparts, Jacques Brugnon, Henri Cochet, and René Lacoste, Borotra was often referred to as one of 'The Four Musketeers' named after the 1921 film adaptation of Alexandre Dumas' novel of the same name. During the 1920s and 1930s, the four men won a total of twenty Grand Slam singles titles, as well as twenty-three Grand Slam doubles titles. Collectively they were responsible for leading France to six consecutive Davis Cup titles between 1927 and 1932.

After his demobilisation in 1919, Borotra had remained on the French Army's reserve list. As trouble brewed throughout Europe and war became more and more likely, he was once again called upon to assist his country in its hour of need, and he willingly did so as part of the French Army's 232nd Divisional Heavy Artillery Regiment. Despite fighting a gallant and heroic defence at Sedan in May 1940, Borotra and most of his men quickly found themselves surrounded and isolated by German forces. Borotra was one of the lucky ones who managed to escape, and although he had planned to make his way to England, it was a journey that he never made, due to other wartime events that were beyond his control.

The same year, 1940, he agreed to become the Director of the Commission of General Education and Sports for the new Pétain-led Vichy government of France, soon after it was formed in June 1940. Despite this he was no great lover of the German authorities and what they stood for, and he was not afraid to hide his views or opinions. Borotra's disagreeable and cavalier attitude towards the

Nazis greatly annoyed them; the more opportunities they gave him to show his approval of Vichy France's collaboration with the occupying Nazi forces, the more he refused to do so. This included refusing to direct the youth of France in the equivalent of Germany's Hitler Youth. He also alienated himself with sections of France's female population when he prohibited them from taking part in competitions for cycling and football.

The longer he continued his acts of non-compliance, the more likely his arrest became. Finally, on 22 November 1942, as he was about to board a train in Paris, he was arrested by members of the Gestapo and would spend the rest of the war in captivity, the last year of which at Itter Castle.

Édouard Daladier

Although already a French politician before the start of the First World War, and despite the fact he was already 30 years of age when it began in earnest, Daladier served in the French Army and saw action on the Western Front. In 1916 he fought with the 209th French Infantry Regiment at Verdun, where his inspirational conduct led to him being promoted in the field as a lieutenant, having begun the war as an ordinary conscript. He later received a further promotion and ended the war as a captain, having also been awarded both the Légion d'honneur and the Croix de Guerre. Having been demobbed at the end of the war, he once again returned to politics.

Physically, Daladier was an intimidating character, with a facial expression not many could engage with for any prolonged period of time, mainly because of his cold-eyed look with a steely and dogged determination. He was a powerfully built individual, with broad shoulders and a neck so big he was often referred to as the 'bull of Vaucluse' (the name of the area in the south-eastern region of Provence-Alpes-Côte d'Azur he represented in the French Parliament).

Having taken office on 10 April 1938, Daladier was the Prime Minister of France when the Second World War broke out. This was his third, and final, time as the French Prime Minister, having first held the position between 31 January and 26 October 1933, and 30 January and 9 February 1934.

On 30 September 1938, he was in Munich with Neville Chamberlain, Adolf Hitler and Benito Mussolini when all four men signed the Munich Agreement, which provided cession to Nazi Germany of the Sudeten German territory of Czechoslovakia. This was despite the fact that France and Czechoslovakia had a military pact in place which had been signed in 1925. Czechoslovakia was not invited to the meeting in Munich, nor was it a signatory of the agreement. Hitler announced that the Sudetenland would be his last territorial claim in northern Europe. Somewhat naively, both Chamberland and Daladier believed him, but in fairness most European nations were glad of the agreement as they saw it as a way to guarantee peace throughout Europe.

Daladier was openly damming of Nazi Germany and did not shy away from saying so. This was made abundantly clear in a message he delivered to the people of France in a radio broadcast on 29 January 1940: 'For us, there is more to do than merely win the war. We shall win it, but we must also win a victory far greater than that of arms. In this world of masters and slaves, which those madmen who rule at Berlin are seeking to forge, we must also save liberty and human dignity.'

Daladier continued as Prime Minister until 21 March 1940, when he resigned due to France's failure to assist Finland after it had been invaded by Russia on 30 November 1939.

The man who replaced Daladier as the French Prime Minister was Paul Reynaud, who would also be one of the captives held at Itter Castle. Despite Daladier's resignation as Prime Minister, he still held the position of Minister of Defence until the French Army were defeated at the Battle of Sedan by German forces from Army Group A, a massive force that consisted of more than forty-five divisions. On this occasion, Daladier had no time to resign his remaining government position and was instead replaced when the incoming Prime Minister assumed the role.

After the Fall of France in May/June 1940, Daladier made his way to French Morocco, where the French government in exile aimed to operate from. But as Daladier quickly discovered, this was not to be a place of sanctuary for him. Instead, he was arrested and tried for treason by the Vichy government, who controlled the southern part of France, headed by Marshal Philippe Pétain, who took the decision to collaborate with Nazi Germany.

From the time of his arrest to when he eventually appeared in court to face his accusers, Daladier was held at the old French military barracks at Fort du Portalet, situated in the Aspe Valley in the Pyrenees mountains. His imprisonment was not a lonely one, as he had plenty of company in the form of other well-known French luminaries such as Léon Blum, Paul Reynard and Maurice Gamelin, to name but a few.

Between 19 February and 21 May 1943, Daladier found himself a defendant in the Riom Trial. This was an attempt by the Vichy government, to make the leaders of the French Third Republic, the French government in charge at the time of the outbreak of the war, officially responsible for France's defeat at the hands of Nazi Germany. However, this was more about internal French politics as the government of the French Third Republic, which had come to power in 1936, was an alliance of left-wing socialist and communist political parties.

There was a lot resting on the case, and to support their prosecution, Pétain, and the Vichy government had the additional fact of being able to highlight that France had been the initial aggressor when it declared war on Germany on 3 September 1939.

The case, which became a long, drawn-out affair, did not quite go according to plan, as the charges against the defendants could not be proven and it was officially abandoned on 21 May 1943.

For Daladier, however, this did not mean freedom. Having been handed over to the Nazis, he was deported to Germany where he was imprisoned at Buchenwald concentration camp. He was held there until May 1943 when he was moved to Itter Castle. It is not recorded what, if anything, Daladier was told about the reasons behind why he was being moved to both Buchenwald and Itter Castle, or what he thought would happen to him on his arrival.

Paul Reynaud

Paul Reynaud had been educated at the prestigious Cambridge University in England and was the French Prime Minister at the time of the Fall of France in June 1940. He was held at the castle, along with his long-time mistress, Christiane Mabire.

Reynaud had been a prominent politician in the interwar years in France as a member of the Democratic Alliance Party, which is best described as a centre-right party, and was seen by many to be a maverick, speaking his mind as he saw things rather than towing the party line.

In 1932, whilst Minister of Justice in the French government, he opposed the decisions made as part of the Munich Agreement, which in essence ceded the Sudeten area of Czechoslovakia to Nazi Germany, despite the

1924 Alliance Agreement and the 1925 Military Pact that were in place between France and Czechoslovakia.

At the beginning of the Second World War, French politicians were far from in agreement about what course of action should be taken. There were those, mainly from the political French Right, who felt that Joseph Stalin and the Soviet Union posed a greater military threat than Adolf Hitler and the Nazi Party did. Édouard Daladier, however, saw it the other way round, and believed that Germany posed the greater and more imminent threat to France. The relevance of Daladier's view of the situation was important because it ultimately led to Paul Reynaud becoming the Prime Minister of France.

The Winter War, also known as the First Soviet-Finnish War, took place between 30 November 1939 and 13 March 1940. The French were connected to this war because Daladier refused to assist Finland militarily, with either men or equipment. The knock-on effect of this decision was that Finland was left with no other option but to sue for peace. This in turn cost Daladier his job as Prime Minister, and he was forced from office. Two days later, Paul Reynaud became the new Prime Minister of France, but it was far from being a unanimous decision. The Chamber of Deputies voted him into power by just one vote, the small margin of victory coming about because nearly all the Deputies from his own party abstained themselves voting. The lack of unity amongst French political parties ultimately resulted in instability in Reynaud's government, with many on the Right wanting France to take the fight to the Soviet Union and not Germany.

Matters were made worse because Daladier, Reynaud's predecessor, was made Minister of National Defence and War by the Chamber of Deputies, in what can only be described as an extremely confusing and unhelpful decision, seeing that Daladier had been so indecisive militarily when he had refused to assist Finland in the fight with Soviet forces when in power himself; a decision which had seen him replaced as Prime Minister by Reynaud. Why it was suddenly thought that Daladier would now be able to make sound military decisions, is unclear.

On 10 May 1940, just two months after Reynaud came to power, Germany began its invasion of France and after just five days, it became clear that Reynaud and France were fighting a losing battle. By the end of May it was becoming abundantly clear that France had almost been overcome by German forces, and within the French government there were vastly differing views as to what their next move should be. Reynaud met with British Prime Minister Winston Churchill in London on 26 May and informed him that he had no intention of seeking a separate peace settlement with Nazi Germany, but added that if he was replaced as Prime Minister, he believed there were those in the French government who would be more than happy to seek favourable terms from the Germans in any subsequent negotiated settlement between the two nations.

If the situation was not difficult enough for Reynaud, it worsened greatly when Italy entered the war on the side of Germany on 10 June 1940. Although Reynaud wanted to continue the fight, he was fast becoming a solitary voice, with even his own Commander-in-Chief, General Weygand, demanding that he seek an armistice with the Germans. This in turn was not a decision which General Charles de Gaulle agreed with, to such a degree that he encouraged Reynaud to remove Weygand from his post.

Time was fast running out for Reynaud. His position as Prime Minister and any remaining options that he had were worsening by the day. An urgent conference was arranged between the British and French governments which took place between 11 and 12 June at the Chateau du Muguet, at Briare in northern France. Winston Churchill tried his utmost to encourage the French to remain in the fight against Germany, but even his usual powers of persuasion were clearly falling on deaf ears, especially those of the French Deputy Prime Minister Marshal Pétain. By 13 June, even Reynaud himself was wavering and he asked Churchill to be released from the agreement he had made with Neville Chamberlain in March 1940, in which he had agreed not to seek a separate armistice with Germany. By this time the pressure on Reynaud to sue for peace was immense, with both Pétain and Weygand in favour of such an action. Realising there was little he could do to prevent his nation's capitulation, Reynaud tendered his resignation later the same day, but it was refused by French President Albert Lebrun. Although this would potentially have been the opportunity for Lebrun to replace Reynaud with Pétain and seek an armistice with Germany, it was almost as if nobody within the French political arena wanted to be the individual who went down in history as the one who agreed to such a telling decision. It was not until the evening of 16 June that Reynaud was able to persuade Lebrun to accept his resignation. His relief must have been palpable. It must have felt like the weight of the world had been removed from his shoulders.

Lebrun appointed Pétain as Reynaud's replacement as Prime Minister, and it was he who subsequently signed the armistice with Germany on 22 June.

On 28 June, having left Hotel Splendid in Bordeaux, where he had met with Charles de Gaulle, Reynaud drove towards the south of France, possibly on his way to Marseille, from where he may have intended to take a boat to North Africa. Reynaud also had a holiday home at Grès, Hérault, while his daughter had a home at Sainte-Maxime, both of which were possible destinations he could have initially been heading for.

The small Renault Juvaquatre Reynaud was travelling in inexplicably left the road and crashed into a tree at La Peyrade, near Sete. Hélène de Portes, a woman with whom Reynaud had been acquainted with since the early 1920s, and who had been his mistress since 1938, was killed in the crash, her injuries being so bad that she was almost decapitated. Reynaud survived, sustaining only minor head injuries, although these were still sufficiently serious enough to result in him being detained in a nearby hospital at Montpellier.

Reynaud knew he was in a precarious position if he remained in France. Unbeknown to him, Pétain had already ordered that he was to be arrested when he was discharged from his hospital bed. Once in custody, he was driven to the Aspe Valley in the French Pyrenees and imprisoned at Fort du Portalet.

In 1942, Pétain handed Reynaud over to the Germans, who initially imprisoned him at the Sachsenhausen concentration camp before he was eventually transferred to Itter Castle. He was joined there by his new mistress, Christiane Mabire, in 1943, who saw it as her duty to be by his side.

General Maxime Weygand

Weygand, who was a former Commander-in-Chief of the French Army, was at Itter Castle with his wife. Belgian by birth, he was born in Brussels on 21 January 1867.

There is much confusion and uncertainty surrounding Weygand's actual parentage. When he was just 6 years of age, he became a member of the household of financier David de Léon Cohen, a close friend of Leopold II, King of the Belgians, and one of the men rumoured to have been Weygand's father. To confuse matters even further, on reaching his eighteenth birthday, he was legally acknowledged as the son of François-Joseph Weygand, an accountant who worked for David de Léon Cohen, although there is no known explanation as to how or why that scenario came to be. Hence how he ended up with his surname. This also had the added bonus of providing him with French citizenship.

Weygand graduated from the French military academy *École spéciale militaire de Saint-Cyr*, in 1887. As a foreign student he was enrolled under the name of Maxime de Nimal, although once again there is no known explanation as to why he required a pseudonym.

After graduating from the academy, his first posting was to a cavalry regiment and he later went on to become an instructor at the prestigious *École de cavalerie*, located at Saumur in western France.

Weygand was quite clearly an impressive young man who had a natural flare for military tactics and strategies. This was proven by his attendance at the *Centre des Hautes Etudes Militaire*, a French military school, where what could best be described as advanced theories on military strategies were taught, but only for those officers who had previously taken and passed staff college, which Weygand had not.

His involvement in the First World War was largely as a staff officer to General Ferdinand Foch, who was also seen as a leading military theorist. Foch also had a reputation during the early years of the war of being a leader who could be quite reckless, and cared little, or not at all, for the wellbeing or lives of the men who served under him. In March 1918 he became the Supreme Allied Commander-in-Chief, and not only effectively dealt with the German Spring Offensive of 1918, but launched such a well detailed counterattack that in essence, it won the war for the Allied powers.

On 7 November 1917, the Allied Supreme War Council, which had been the brainchild of the then British Prime Minister David Lloyd George, was established. Each nation nominated what was known as a Permanent Military Representative (PMR), and the man chosen to represent the interests of France was Weygand, but he was not the new French Prime Minister Clemenceau's preferred choice, which had been Foch. In keeping with the importance of his new position, Weygand was promoted to the rank of general de division (Major General).

It was Foch who signed the Armistice for the French on 11 November 1918, with Weygand, who by now held the rank of general de brigade, sitting immediately to his left.

In 1931 Weygand became the Chief of Staff of the French Army, before retiring in 1935 when he was 68. In August 1939, the French Prime Minister Édouard Daladier, who was also later one of those in captivity at Itter Castle, recalled Weygand to active service. Just nine months later, in May 1940, matters became even more interesting when the Supreme Commander of all French military forces, Maurice Gamelin, another held at Itter, was dismissed from his position and replaced by none other than Maxime Weygand.

As if having to fight Germany was not difficult enough, on 10 June matters worsened when Italian forces under the command of Benito Mussolini also decided that the time was right to invade France. For Weygand, who was by all accounts a practical man, this was the final straw. As far as he was concerned, the omens were not good at all and demanded the new French Prime Minister Reynaud, another captive at Itter, that he should seek an armistice with Germany. By 15 June the French government had moved to Bordeaux, where a cabinet meeting was held to discuss what course of action they should take, knowing full well that as they did so, their forces were being totally over-run and could not continue the fight for much longer. Although not a member of the French Cabinet, it would appear that Weygand played a direct part in the decision to seek an armistice with the Germans, rather than agree to another suggestion which was to order all French forces to lay down their arms.

The following day, Reynaud resigned as Prime Minister and the President of France, Albert Lubrun, made the historic and somewhat divisive decision to ask Pétain to replace him and form a new government, which Weygand joined as the new Minister of Defence.

The armistice with Germany was finally signed on board a train carriage at Compiègne Forest on the evening of 22 June 1940, a location specifically chosen by Hitler because it was the same location in 1918 where Germany had signed the armistice to end the First World War. The same train carriage was used for both occasions.

With Pétain as Prime Minister, the new government of Vichy France came into being. Weygand was appointed as the Delegate-General in French North Africa in

September 1940 and it was whilst holding this position that he showed what could be described as his 'true colours'. He was directly involved in the deportation of anyone who was identified as being an opponent of Vichy France to camps located in both Algeria and Morocco. Those deported also included a number of Jews. But he did not stop there. Foreign refugees who were in France legally, but who did not have a job, were also in danger of ending up in a concentration camp, despite having committed absolutely no crime whatsoever. Next it was the turn of the education system which came to Weygand's attention. Without either the approval or bequest of Pétain, Weygand in effect had all Jewish students and primary school children moved out of schools. The question here is what constituted collaboration, as Weygand was in support of what he called 'limited' collaboration, but surely collaboration in any form with Nazi Germany was simply that, collaboration. Hitler did not see it that way as he expected complete and unconditional collaboration, and he for one was unhappy with Weygand's efforts in North Africa to such a degree that he wanted him dismissed from the Vichy government and returned to France. In late 1942, Weygand was arrested and eventually ended up as a detainee at Itter Castle.

After having been released from the castle in May 1945, he was arrested for having been a collaborator and held at the Val-de-Grâce military hospital in Paris, which was used both as a hospital and a prison during and immediately after the end of the Second World War.

Despite his wartime indiscretions as part of Pétain's Vichy government, he was never prosecuted and was officially cleared by the French government in 1948. He received a number of decorations for his wartime involvement, including medals from France and seven other countries, including the United Kingdom, which awarded him the Knight Commander of the Order of St. Michael and St. George for chivalry.

General Maurice Gustave Gamelin

Gamelin was a former Chief of Staff until his suppression by General Weygand in 1940.

By the time of the First World War, Gamelin had already served in the French Army for twenty-three years, having volunteered as a soldier on 19 October 1891, before going on to study at both the *École spéciale militaire de Saint-Cyr*, and the *École supérieure de guerre*, where he was recognised by his instructors as being both intelligent and industrious; an individual who was destined to be a leader. In 1906 he published a book entitled *Philosophical Study of the Art of War*, which was well received by military experts of the time, leading to the belief that he would go on to become a major military strategist.

Gamelin learned much from his involvement in the First World War, which began as a member of the general staff of renowned French Army General, Joseph Joffre. He was involved in the planning for the Battle of the Marne, between 5 and 12 September 1914, resulting in the defeat of German forces by a combined British and French force, which numbered more than 1 million men. As a Lieutenant Colonel he saw action at the Battle of Alsace, also known as the Battle of Mulhouse, in August 1914, the Battle of Le Linge, between July and October 1915, and the Battle of the Somme, which began on 1 July 1916. From April 1917 to the end of the war he commanded the French 11th Infantry Division.

He remained in the French Army during the post war years and at the outbreak of the Second World War was the Commander-in-Chief of the French Army, with a reputation for being one of the best generals in Europe, even by senior officers of the German Wehrmacht.

It would be fair to say that things did not quite go according to plan as far as Gamelin's decision making was concerned. His strategy was more a case of 'wait and see', meaning that it was based more on defence than attack, and by the time he did decide to react, it was already too late, resulting in French forces and elements of the British Expeditionary Force being quickly outflanked by the rapidly advancing German Panzer divisions in May 1940. It could be said that one of his glaring mistakes was in his belief that once German forces had managed to make their way through the dense forests of the Ardennes, they would automatically make their way to Paris to capture the nation's capital. But they did not. Instead, they made their way towards the coast. Gamelin was relieved of his position on 18 May by Prime Minister Paul Reynaud.

At the time he was liberated from Itter Castle, Gamelin was already 72 years of age. For him there was to be no return to military life, or involvement in politics. Instead, he chose to write and publish his memoirs. He died on 18 April 1958 in Paris, aged 85.

François de La Rocque

De La Rocque, like many of his contemporaries, had served in the French military during the First World War. He had graduated from the *École spéciale militaire de Saint-Cyr* in 1907, and by the outbreak of the First World War was serving in Morocco under the command of General Hubert Lyautey, and by 1916 was the officer of native affairs. It was during this time that he was badly wounded in action, which resulted in him having to be repatriated back home to France. After making a full recovery, de La Rocque volunteered to serve on the Western Front, a decision which saw him placed in charge of a unit during the Battle of the Somme. After the war he remained in the French Army, having reached the rank of Lieutenant Colonel, before eventually resigning in 1927.

In 1929 he joined the *Croix de Feu*, a French right wing fascist party, which had been formed in 1927 by a group of army veterans who had been awarded the Croix de Guerre during the First World War. By 1930 he became the party's leader, a position he held for the following six years. During his time in charge of the *Croix de Feu*, de La

Rocque found himself up against Édouard Daladier. This confrontation came about on the evening of 6 February 1934, when demonstrations organised by a number of far-right groups took place in Paris. The intention was to converge on the Palais Bourbon, home of the country's National Assembly, the lower legislative chamber of the French Parliament.

The resulting riots had the desired effect and the following day Daladier and his government resigned.

De La Rocque later formed the *Parti Social Français*, or the French Social Party in 1936 after the Popular Front government dissolved all the country's far-right groups.

It would be fair to describe de La Rocque as a rather complex character, who was prone to changing his mind, sometimes to dramatic degrees. After the signing of the armistice between German and French officials in June 1940, he was initially in favour of the 'principle of collaboration', but by 1942 his rhetoric was the complete opposite. In October 1940 he was talking and writing about 'the Jewish question in Metropolitan France and North Africa', but by 1941 his views and opinions had become more anti-German in their tone. By the end of 1942, along with other members of the *Parti Social Français*, he formed the *Réseau Klan* resistance movement, and was against young French men being sent to Germany to work as forced labour as part of the Nazi war effort.

On 30 January 1943, the *Milice française*, more commonly referred to as simply *la Milice*, was formed by the Vichy government. It was a political paramilitary group whose purpose was to hunt down and fight against the French Resistance. De La Rocque banned any of his members from joining *la Milice.*

De La Rocque was arrested on 9 March 1943 in Clermont-Ferrand by the *Sicherheitspolizei* or security police. Initially held at Eisenberg Castle, in what is now the Czech Republic, he was later transferred to Itter Castle. Because of ill health he was sent for hospital treatment in Innsbruck in March 1945, where he remained until 8 May 1945 after being freed by advancing US soldiers. He was returned to his home in France the following day but was arrested and placed under house arrest. He died whilst undergoing surgery in a Paris hospital on 28 April 1946.

Michel William Benjamin Clémenceau

Clémenceau was the son, and youngest of three children, of the great French statesman, Georges Benjamin Clémenceau, who twice served as the Prime Minister of France. During his second appointment, he also held the position of Minister of War. He was also appointed as President of the Paris Peace Conference which took place at the Palace of Versailles in June 1919. One of the major decisions that came out of the conference was the Treaty of Versailles.

Michel Clémenceau's mother, Mary Elizabeth Plummer, was an American who attended the prestigious Aiken Seminary girls' school in Stamford, Connecticut, where Georges Clémenceau taught French. He had fled

France in 1859 during the reign of Napoleon III for political reasons.

Michel's elder brother, William Benjamin Clémenceau, had been a Colonel in the French Army during the First World War, whilst his sister, Madeleine, had also served her country as a Red Cross Nurse.

By the time of his incarceration at Itter Castle, Michel Clémenceau was already in his 60s. He had followed in his father's footsteps in becoming a politician, but he was also an engineer and a qualified pharmacist. He was a married man who had wed three times, the last occasion being in 1963, when he was 89 years of age, the year before he died.

Léon Jouhaux

Léon Jouhaux was a French Labour leader, born in Paris in July 1879 into a staunch and active workers' union family.

His grandfather had fought in the French Revolution of 1848, also known as the February Revolution, when civil unrest broke out across Paris because of a government crackdown on political meetings. The revolution led to the abdication of King Louis Philippe and the foundation of the French Second Republic.

Jouhaux's father followed in his own father's footsteps by being part of the Commune who briefly took control of Paris in the aftermath of the Franco-Prussian War, which took place between July 1870 and January 1871.

Léon Jouhaux had been involved in the union movement since he had started work at a local match factory in Aubervilliers, a suburb of Paris, aged just 16. He had been forced to end his secondary education at the *Lycée Colbert* because his father, who also worked at the same factory, had decided to go on strike and in doing so was unable to earn a wage to provide for his family. His father eventually lost his sight as a direct result of long-term exposure to white phosphorus that was used extensively in the manufacture of the matches.

In 1900, when he was 21, Jouhaux took part in his first real strike in protest against the factory's use of phosphorus. The outcome of his actions, and those of the others who took part in the strike, resulted in him losing his job. It also marked him as a troublemaker, which in turn made it difficult for him to find another full time, regular job, as prospective employers were concerned that he might try to cause disaffection amongst their work force. He did, however, find work doing jobs which only sustained him for a matter of days, before he moved on to another job, a sequence that was repeated time and again. All the work was of a menial nature and not necessarily what he wanted to do, but needs must. Whilst flitting from job to job he took the opportunity to continue his education, which included attending the local *Université Populaire* at Aubervilliers.

Fortunately for Jouhaux, he had not been forgotten by his colleagues at the union, for whom he had gone out on strike, and with their help and assistance he was given his job back at the match factory in Aubervilliers. This new beginning for him, this second chance, was the start of his life as a union leader, and in July 1909 he was appointed as the General Secretary of the powerful and influential *Confédération Générale du Travail* (CGT) union, a position, which despite his incarceration, he held until 1947. It was because of his longevity and position in the CGT that he earned his nickname of 'the General'.

Jouhaux was first and foremost a patriot and was against the German occupation of his country at a time when being openly anti-Nazi was an extremely dangerous course of action to take. In turn, the Nazis were no great admirer of him; as an important and relatively powerful union representative, they perceived him as a threat to their regime. They were also aware that Jouhaux was a member of the French Resistance. Consequently, he was arrested in December 1941, but instead of killing him, as might have been expected as a high-value prisoner, he was held under house arrest instead. This situation continued for more than a year before it was decided to send him to the notorious German concentration camp at Buchenwald. From there he was later moved to Itter Castle, where he remained until he was liberated in May 1945. Despite being 66 and having been a prisoner of the Nazi regime for more than two years, Jouhaux had somehow managed to remain in good health.

During his imprisonment at Itter Castle, Jouhaux was joined by his secretary and long-term mistress Augustine Brüchlen. She had begun working for Jouhaux as an interpreter when she was in her early twenties. A clever woman who was able to speak French, German and English, as time went by her relationship with Jouhaux changed from been a purely working one, to a romantic one as well. Even after Jouhaux's arrest in December 1941, he and Brüchlen were still able to see each other.

Brüchlen was herself arrested in January 1943 and held under house arrest at the same location as her lover. But just two months later, and without any prior warning, Jouhaux was suddenly moved to Itter Castle. The Gestapo did not tell Brüchlen where he had been moved to or the reason why. Rather than just sit back and accept the situation she found herself in, however, she repeatedly pushed the Gestapo to allow her to be reunited with Jouhaux. Just under three months later, her wish was granted when she joined him at Itter Castle.

In 1951, Jouhaux was awarded the Nobel Peace Prize 'for having devoted his life to the fight against war through the promotion of social justice and brotherhood among men and all nations'. He died in Paris on 28 April 1954, aged 74.

Marie-Agnes Caroline Julie Calliau and Alfred Georges Marie Ghislain Joseph Cailliau

During the Second World War the name Marie-Agnes Calliau would not have been known to many people outside of France if it had not been for the fact that she was the elder sister of the man in charge of the Free

French forces, General Charles de Gaulle. Indeed, it was her direct connection to him that was the only reason why her and her husband, Alfred, were detained by the Nazis.

Marie-Agnes and Alfred, who was a Belgian engineer, married on 18 January 1910. The couple had seven children: a daughter and six sons. Four of their sons, Josephe, Charles, Henri, and Michel, all enlisted in the French Army at the beginning of the war to help save their country from the tyranny of the invading German forces. Their second eldest son, Charles, was killed in action at Charleroi, Belgium, on 10 May 1940, the very first day of the German invasion of Western Europe. Their eldest son, Josephe, and his younger brother Henri were amongst Allied forces who were forced back to the Channel ports by the rapidly advancing German forces and managed to escape to England during the evacuations at Dunkirk. Michel, although alive, was not so fortunate. Along with a number of his colleagues, and despite fighting bravely, he was captured during fighting at Domeray in Lorraine and was sent to the Stalag XI B camp, which was situated at Fallingbostel in Germany. During the Battle of France, an estimated 1.8 million French soldiers were captured and deported to Germany where they were made to work in support of the German war effort, mostly in either agriculture or industry.

This would have been a difficult time for Marie-Agnes and Alfred, because although they were aware of the death of their son Charles, they would have been oblivious to the whereabouts of Josephe, Henri and Michel, let alone whether they were alive or dead.

Both Marie-Agnes and Alfred became involved with the French Resistance, but although they were arrested in April 1943, it was not because of their clandestine actions as they may have at first believed to have been the case, but because Marie-Agnes was the sister of General Charles de Gaulle. What better bargaining chip could Nazi Germany have possibly had with France and her allies?

After initial questioning, the couple were detained at the notorious Fresnes Prison, which is situated to the south of Paris, where during the Second World War a number of detainees were tortured and murdered.

Marie-Agnes and Alfred only arrived at Itter Castle in April 1945. It is known that in January 1944 Alfred was being held at Buchenwald concentration camp, and that Marie-Agnes joined him there the following month. Between their initial detention in April 1943 and incarceration at Fresnes, and before arriving at Buchenwald, they were held at other locations in Germany.

Moving the couple to Itter Castle so late on in the war is an interesting decision. By the time of their arrival, the Nazis were in full retreat; the war was all but lost and American and Soviet forces were racing each other to be the first to reach Berlin. With the war in its final weeks, it is difficult to see what was to be gained by sending Marie-Agnes and Alfred to Itter Castle.

Marcel Granger (Relative of General Henri Honoré Giraud)

Marcel Granger is quite possibly one of the least important French individuals who were held captive at Itter Castle. Indeed, it would be fair to say that he was as unimportant to the French people as General Henri Honoré Giraud was important. In fact, the only reason he had been held hostage there was because of his family connection to General Giraud. That was it, pure and simple.

History has not recorded very much about this man at all. Once liberated from Itter Castle, photographs of all the other French dignitaries were taken and appeared in numerous newspapers and magazines around the world. The only person for whom no such image appears is Marcel Granger. It is known that along with all the other French prisoners who had been held at the castle, he was initially taken to Paris, but after that the man who Édouard Daladier described in his post-war memoire, *Prison Journal 1940-1945*, as 'a fine man, highly patriotic and brave, and a wonderful example of the average French man', simply disappeared off the face of the earth.

It shows the significance of what the Germans thought of Giraud if they decided there was a value in incarcerating Marcel Granger at Itter Castle.

General Giraud was the man in charge of Free French Forces during the Second World War. He had the unique claim to fame of not only having served his country in both the First and Second World Wars, but he had also been captured and then subsequently escaped on both occasions.

He had also served in the French Army during the interwar years, seeing action in the Rif War in Morocco after France had entered the war on the side of the Spanish in 1925, for which he was awarded the Legion d'honneur.

At the beginning of the Second World War, Giraud was a member of France's Superior War Council and was not afraid to speak up if he felt it necessary to do so, as Charles de Gaulle discovered when the two men disagreed on certain military tactics that each of them felt should have been deployed by French forces.

On 10 May 1940, Giraud was placed in charge of the French 7th Army and deployed with his men to the Netherlands. Three days later he and his troops were set up in defensive positions at Breda, in the south of the country, in an effort to try to delay the German advance. On 19 May he was with his men whilst engaged in fighting German forces that were advancing through the Ardennes. Having decided to take a group of his men on a reconnaissance patrol to locate the enemies' exact positions and numbers, he was captured at the town of Wassigny in north-east France. Giraud's capture left him in a precarious situation, because in earlier fighting he had ordered the execution of two German soldiers who had been caught in civilian clothing, and who he took to be acting as saboteurs. He was placed before a German military court martial but was acquitted and incarcerated in Königstein Castle near Dresden, which at the time was being used as a **POW** camp for those deemed by the Nazis to be high value prisoners.

As an officer and a gentleman, Giraud was never going to just sit back and enjoy the comparative luxury of life as a high-ranking **POW**. As might be expected of any good officer, he deemed it his duty to escape, and on 17 April 1942, he did just that.

Giraud certainly did not waste his time whilst in captivity. He learnt to speak, read, and write German to a more than competent level. Having managed to acquire a map of the castle's surrounding area, he memorised it in minute detail. The degree of planning which he put into his escape plan was such that it took him two years to finalise. Having said that, there was nothing complicated about how the plan was to be executed. In essence he threw a 150 feet rope made up of a number of different items out of one of the castle's upper windows, climbed down it, and escaped into the surrounding countryside dressed in civilian clothes and with his trademark moustache shaved off. Once he had made it out of the castle, he made his way to Schandau, Saxony, a distance of about 6 miles.

Although not by the Germans, Giraud's escape plans were known by the Allied authorities, and to assist him the best that they could, an agent of the British Special Operations Executive (SOE), was sent to Schandau to meet with him. It was a meeting Giraud needed to make because not only did the agent hand over a new set of clothes, money, and a map, but more importantly he provided him with important travel and identity papers.

Having boarded a train, Giraud cautiously made his way towards the Swiss border. It would have been a dangerous journey knowing that he could be captured at any moment, not knowing who else was on the train, or if they were just a member of the public or a Gestapo officer who was hunting him down.

To be extra careful, Giraud did not remain on the train until it had reached the German-Swiss border, as he did not want any problems with German border guards, who by then would have been alerted to his escape from Königstein Castle. Instead, he alighted from the train a couple of miles back and crossed into Switzerland by making his way across the Alps, where he bumped into a couple of Swiss soldiers. Having told them who he was and how he had escaped from a German POW camp, the two soldiers took him to the nation's capital. From there he made his way back to France.

From what he had seen of the war, Giraud had formed the opinion that the Allies were going to be the victors; an opinion which he was more than happy to voice and share with Marshal Pétain and the Vichy government. He even went as far as to suggest that all of France should resist the German occupation of their nation. Although they did not agree with what he had to say, they refused Germany's request to return Giraud.

Ultimately, Giraud was a loyal Frenchman who categorically refused to cooperate with Nazi Germany; an approach that was not received at all well by the occupying powers of his country. Heinrich Himmler was certainly not impressed with him, far from it, in fact. He was so incensed that he ordered the Gestapo not only to try to kill him, but also to arrest any members of his family they could find, a directive which ultimately resulted in seventeen of them being arrested.

Word of Giraud's disillusionment with the Nazis and France's decision not to fight back soon reached the ears of British and American military intelligence, who, having spotted an opportunity, were quick to make contact with him. With the Allies planning landings in North Africa, where Morocco and Algeria had been colonised by the French, Giraud was more than happy to assist, but his help came at a price. His agreement to help was conditional on only American troops being involved in the invasion, as like a number of his fellow French officers, he was no great lover of the British. He also wanted assurances that a French officer would be in overall command of the operation; something Eisenhower and the Americans would ultimately never acquiesce to, even though to ensure his assistance with the operation, they made it sound like they would. Giraud saw the latter request as an extremely important one, as he felt without it, France's authority in the region could be well and truly undermined.

The Allied invasion of North Africa, Operation *Torch*, finally began on 8 November 1942, but it went ahead not without its problems. The best that America could offer Giraud was that he would be in command 'as soon as possible', causing him to counter with a demand for a written agreement that he would be in command within

48 hours of the initial landings. Just one day before the operation got under way, Eisenhower informed Giraud that he would only be in command of French troops and asked him to order his men to join up with Allied forces. Giraud was far from happy, as he had expected to be in overall command of the operation. Initially he refused Eisenhower's request, stating he would only be involved if his demands were met in full, and that 'his honour would be tarnished' if he was not. He did not just want to be a 'mere spectator' in events, which is what he believed he would be if he was not in overall command.

André François-Poncet

André François-Poncet, born in June 1887, was a French politician and diplomat. During the early years of the First World War, he had served as a Lieutenant in the French Army on the Western Front, but in 1917 found himself redeployed to a non-combat role in the Press Office of the French Embassy in Bern, Switzerland. This was not as unusual a posting as it might first appear, as during his student years at university he had studied both journalism and German studies.

Between August 1931 and October 1938, he was the French Ambassador to Germany, which gave him a front row seat not only in relation to the rise of Adolf Hitler and the Nazi Party, but as to their intentions towards their European neighbours and the Jews of Europe. Quite remarkably, the French government chose to ignore numerous warnings François-Poncet gave about what he believed Hitler's real long-term intentions were throughout his time in Berlin.

As would be expected of a competent ambassador, part of his role required him to forge good working relationships with his host government. Such was his professional reputation that when it came time for him to leave his position in Berlin, he was invited to the *Kehlsteinhaus*, better known as the Eagle's Nest, near to the town of Berchtesgaden in south-east Germany, by Adolf Hitler. Although an official meeting, which took place on 18 October 1938, it was also quite informal, with François-Poncet conversing with Hitler in immaculate German, as they ate and drank with each other. Their meeting had taken place less than a month after the Munich Agreement, which had been signed on 30 September.

From Berlin, François-Poncet was not sent back to Paris but to Rome, where he took up the role as the new French Ambassador to Italy, which by now was under the leadership of the Fascist dictator Benito Mussolini. It was a difficult time for all concerned and having seen the relationship of Nazi Germany and Fascist Italy develop throughout the 1930s, the eventual outcome would not have come as much of a surprise to François-Poncet, who remained in Rome until Italy's declaration of war on France and Great Britain on 10 June 1940.

After returning to Paris, he was arrested at his home by the Gestapo in 1942, and spent the remainder of the war in custody, much of which was spent at Itter Castle.

François-Poncet became the first French post-war era high-commissioner to the newly formed West Germany in 1949; a position which was elevated to that of Ambassador before he finally left Berlin in 1955.

He wrote a number of non-fiction books, most of which covered the period from when he had been the French Ambassador to Germany throughout the 1930s.

Tadeusz Komorowski

Although clearly not a French dignitary, the Polish Commander-in-Chief General Tadeusz Komorowski, better known by the name Bór-Komorowski (Bór being a reference to his wartime codename) warrants a reference here as he was also held captive by the Germans at Itter Castle for the same reasons as his French counterparts; because it was believed he could be used as a bargaining chip by the Germans, meaning that he was perceived by them as extremely important and highly valuable prisoner.

Bór-Komorowski was born in June 1895 in Khorobriv, which at the time was part of the Austrian partition of Poland, but which is now part of Ukraine. An experienced military man, he first saw action during the First World War as an officer in the Austro-Hungarian Army. After the end of the war, and with the Austro-Hungarian Empire no longer in existence, he became an officer in the Polish Army.

At the outbreak of the Second World War, he took part in the fighting against the invading German Army, and by March 1943 had been promoted to the rank of Brigadier General and had become the commander of the entire Polish Home Army.

It was Komorowski who had given the order for the commencement of the Warsaw Uprising, which began on 1 August 1944 and had been specifically timed to coincide with the retreat of German forces from Poland as the Soviet Red Army chased them back to their homeland. Sadly, for the Polish military and the nation's civilian population, the Soviets did not maintain their advance and stopped on the outskirts of Warsaw. This provided the Germans with some much-needed breathing space and time to consolidate their situation. Rather than continuing to escape and put as much distance between themselves and Soviet forces as was possible, the Germans remained in Warsaw and took on the Polish forces who had been attacking them. The outcome was devastating for the Poles, who were mainly well-organised resistance fighters, as well as the civilian population. Finally, after sixty-three days of fighting, the uprising was over after the Warsaw Home Army surrendered to the attacking German forces by means of a capitulation agreement, part of which included Polish resistance fighters to be treated as prisoners of war, in keeping with the terms laid down by the Geneva Convention, and a guarantee of the safety of Polish civilians. The agreement between the two sides was signed by General Bór-Komorowski and General Erich von dem Bach-Zelewski. The majority of the Home Army soldiers ended up as POWs in camps throughout Germany, whilst the civilian population ended up in concentration camps.

In September 1944, Bór-Komorowski was promoted to General Inspector of the Armed Forces (Polish Commander-in-Chief). He went into internment, initially in Germany at Oflag IV-C, before then being moved to Itter Castle along with his deputy, General Tadeusz Pelczyński.

Liberated at the end of the war, along with the French dignitaries held at Itter Castle, he spent the rest of his life living in London, where he played an active role in Polish émigré circles. From 2 July 1947 to 10 February 1949, he served as Prime Minister of the Polish government-in-exile in London, which no longer had diplomatic recognition from most Western European countries, which was somewhat strange, taking into account the part Poland played in the overall Allied victory.

He wrote and published his account of his wartime experiences in a book entitled, *The Secret Army* (1950). After the war he took up work as an upholsterer. He died aged 71 whilst out hunting in the Welsh town of Buckley and was buried in Gunnersbury Cemetery in London. On 30 July 1994, his ashes were re-buried in the Powazki Military Cemetery in Warsaw, Poland.

The Battle of Itter Castle

Soviet and Bulgarian forces had advanced into Austria, via Hungary, in March 1945, which resulted in the Vienna Offensive beginning on 16 March. German forces were defeated in just four weeks, but this came as no real surprise: Soviet and Bulgarian forces, which totalled 77 divisions, or 1,171,800 men, were up against just 25 German divisions, or 270,000 men. By the end of the fighting, some 30,000 German soldiers had been killed, whilst an estimated 125,000 had been captured.

The only real saving grace for German forces stationed in and around the area of Itter, was that the Soviet and Bulgarian forces were some 264 miles away to the south-west, and much closer to American and French forces, advancing into Austria from Germany.

On 26 April 1945, American forces of the 11th Armored Division had begun their advance into Austria from Germany, followed three days later by those from France. The main disadvantage for the advancing Allied forces was their lack of any up-to-date, first-hand intelligence.

One thing they had absolutely no information about was the importance of Itter Castle and the 'high value' individuals who were incarcerated there.

By the beginning of May 1945, the war in Europe was almost at an end. Men from both sides knew that they were sitting round waiting to be officially informed that the fighting was over and that the Allies had won. For most German military personnel, their main focus was no longer the war, but to ensure that they survived the fighting and became prisoners of the British or Americans rather than the Soviets.

On 3 May, SS-Obersturmbannführer (Lieutenant Colonel) Eduard Weiter, the former Commandant of Dachau concentration camp, died whilst at Itter Castle. The officially accepted story concerning Weiter's death comes from the lips of one of the castle's French prisoners, the politician Paul Reynaud, who stated that a drunken Weiter shot and killed himself whilst outlining the numerous executions he had ordered at Dachau prior to his escape. There is no reason to disbelieve Reynaud's account as he had nothing to gain from making such a bold statement. Weiter undoubtedly knew what his eventual fate would be once captured, and rather than have to suffer the indignity of being hung as a common criminal, he chose to take his own life, and was more able to do so whilst in a drunken state.

By the beginning of May 1945, with advancing American, French, and Russian forces slowly winding their way towards each other, most German soldiers knew the war was over and that for them fighting was no longer a concern; all that mattered now was survival and self-preservation.

One of the Eastern European prisoners who was being used as a worker at Itter Castle was Zvonimir Čučković, a Croatian resistance fighter. On 3 May, with the castle's commanding officer, Sebastian Wimmer, and his guards more concerned about their own wellbeing rather than that of those they were there to keep from escaping, Čučković left the castle, more than likely with Wimmer's permission and agreement, intent on making contact with US troops that were known to be in the area. His aim was to return with them to the castle and rescue those being held there. It was an extremely brave thing for Čučković to do because there were German Wehrmacht soldiers, as well as SS units, roaming the areas surrounding the castle. If he had bumped into any of the fanatical members of the SS, there is every possibility they would have shot him on the spot, and there was no guarantee American forces would have believed his story about Itter Castle.

Logic suggests that Wimmer knew what Čučković was up to. What other reason would he have to let him leave the castle? He appears to have only been concerned about saving his own skin. It makes sense that he wanted American forces at the castle to arrive before he left, that way if the SS had made it into the castle and subsequently killed the French dignitaries, there would have been no dispute about who had killed them. The last thing he would have wanted was to have been put on trial for murders he had not committed.

To support his story, it is believed that Čučković had with him a letter, written in English, asking for assistance to rescue those being held at the castle, which he was to give to the first American soldiers he encountered. His initial plan was to head for the nearby town of Wörgl, which was only about 5 miles away, a distance which would have taken him about ninety minutes to make. But when he arrived at the town's outskirts, he discovered it was still occupied by large numbers of German soldiers. With no obvious way of establishing whether they were members of the regular German Army or SS, he decided to continue his journey and look for help elsewhere. This time, he headed towards Innsbruck, which was nearly 40 miles away to the south-west, but more importantly for him, it would take him further away from German and Soviet forces and closer to the Americans.

After an exhausting walk which had taken him more than ten hours to complete, just outside Innsbruck he finally bumped into American forces, which included men of the 409th Infantry Regiment of the American 103rd Infantry Division, part of the US VI Army Corps. He handed over his letter, which included the names of those who were being held at the castle. Fortunately for Čučković, the Americans believed his story and began arrangements to mount a rescue.

At first light the following morning, men of the American 409th Infantry Regiment set off in a heavily armoured convoy, enroute to rescue those being held captive at Itter Castle. After having travelled less than

20 miles, which was roughly halfway, they reached the Austrian town of Jenbach. In February 1945, just prior to the Allied invasion of Austria and Germany, the railway station at Jenbach was attacked as part of the aerial bombing that was part of Operation *Clarion*, in an attempt at preventing the Germans from using the Austrian rail network to transport troops and equipment. Jenbach was somewhat unique, as it was the only Austrian town that could cater for three different types of rail gauge. The bombing resulted in a number of homes being destroyed and eight civilians being killed.

Up until Jenbach, the American convoy, with Čučković in the lead vehicle, had not encountered any resistance. But no sooner had they left the town than they came under a heavy and sustained artillery bombardment, more than likely by SS troops. Unbeknown to the American convoy, they had inadvertently wandered into an area which had been allocated to the American 36th Division. But rather than receive support from their own comrades, they were rebuked for entering another division's 'area' by their senior officers and recalled back to Innsbruck. Although it is known that Major John T. Kramers, the man in charge of the American convoy, ordered two of his jeeps to continue on towards Itter with Čučković, they never made it to the castle.

Meanwhile, events back at the castle had taken a different turn. Having not heard back from Čučković, the castle's German commander, Sebastien Wimmer, had started to panic. Not knowing what was happening, he knew he had a decision to make: did he stay and risk retribution from the SS if they discovered his apparent willingness to surrender the castle and its occupants to the Americans, or did he make a run for it and hand himself over to the first group of Americans he came across? Fearing he was in mortal danger the longer he remained at the castle, he fled on 3 May, quickly followed by his SS-Totenkopfverbände guards, who were responsible for all Nazi Germany's concentration and extermination camps.

Once Wimmer had left, the castle was in essence taken over by the French prisoners who were being held captive within its walls, who quickly armed themselves with the weapons left behind by the guards.

The prisoners now found themselves in a similar predicament to what Wimmer had found himself in. Did they wait for the Americans to arrive and secure their safety? If they did, they might also place themselves in danger of being captured and more than likely murdered by SS forces who were known to be in the area.

On 4 May, whilst the prisoners were deciding what to do for the best, the castle's Czechoslovakian cook, Andreas Krobot, offered to cycle in to nearby Wörgl with a similar letter to which Čučković had carried with him when he had left the castle looking for help the day before.

Krobot, having bumped into the extremely helpful Major Josef 'Sepp' Gangl, the man who would stand side by side with American soldiers in the eventual fighting at Castle Itter (see Chapter Seven), was then told by him to make his way towards Innsbruck, as the German officer was aware the Americans had already reached that location. Before he had reached his intended destination, Krobot bumped into elements of the 103rd Infantry Division, who listened intently to his story and decided that not only did they believe him, but they agreed to return with him to the castle and help to rescue those French dignitaries who were being held there. Two of the 103rd's officers, Major John Kramers and Lieutenant Eric Lutten, quickly put together a plan, and in just a couple of hours, the two officers, an eight-vehicle convoy, along with a platoon of men from the 411th Infantry Regiment, were on their way to Itter Castle. Despite the obvious potential for some kind of military engagement with German forces, either on the way or when they arrived at the castle, the group also included the well-known Meyer Levin, an American war correspondent and Éric Schwab, a French war photographer.

Levin was also an author who before the war had had several novels published, which were well received in the writing world. During the Second World War he worked with American forces as they made their way across Europe, working for both the Overseas News Agency and the Jewish Telegraphic Agency. After the war he continued with his writing and had a number of other novels published. He died in Jerusalem on 9 July 1981.

Éric Schwab was German by birth, having been born in Hamburg in 1910. His father was French and although his mother was German, she was also Jewish.

Schwab had an interesting war. At the outbreak of hostilities, he was called up into the French Army, but was captured as France capitulated in June 1940. Whilst being transported to Germany as a POW, he managed to escape from the train he was on and make his way back to Paris, where he joined the French Resistance. In September 1944 he began working for the French news agency, Agence France-Presse and was allocated to the United States Army as a war correspondent as they advanced into Germany. It was whilst working in this capacity that he met, became friends with and worked alongside, Meyer Levin.

Both men were with American forces when they started to discover the concentration camps in April 1945. The first one they entered was Ohrdruf, which was one of the satellite camps for the notorious Buchenwald. Schwab took many of the earliest photographs which documented the horrors of what went on inside these camps, shocking the world when they were first published.

It was Schwab who took the photographs of those incarcerated at Itter Castle after it had been liberated. Part of the reason Schwab was working with the Americans was to try to find his mother, who had been interned in an unknown concentration camp by the Nazis earlier in the war. He did not even know if she was alive or dead. After the events at Itter Castle, Schwab continued to work with the advancing American forces, and somewhat miraculously, he discovered his mother Elsbeth, still alive, at Terezin concentration camp in Czechoslovakia.

Just before lunch, not long after having set off from the castle, Krobot arrived at the nearby village of Wörgl. There he bumped into a group of Germans, but thankfully for him not only were they not from the SS, they were German Wehrmacht soldiers who were not supportive of the Nazi cause. Their leader was Wehrmacht Major Joseph 'Sepp' Gangl, who was in the area with a small group of his men to try to protect the local population against the very same SS units that Krobot was most probably praying to avoid.

Not knowing if sending Krobot out to see if he could make contact with American forces in the area would prove fruitful, the French dignitaries who were being held at the castle took what could be described as the somewhat unusual step of placing their trust in the hands of an SS officer, Captain Kurt Siegfried Schrader, who had been staying in Itter whilst he recuperated from his wounds. A kind of friendship, if that is the correct way of describing it, formed between him and some of those who were being held captive. The trust between the two came in the form of having Schrader advise them on how to best defend themselves against an impending attack from colleagues of his in the SS. Maybe like Gangl, he had become disillusioned with the Nazi Party, and knew that it was only a matter of time before the war was lost.

Krobot then explained to Gangl that he had come from Itter Castle and showed him the letter which outlined the details of those being held there and the potential danger they were in when the SS eventually arrived at the castle, which they knew was a matter of when rather than if. It would have been a strange initial conversation between Krobot and Gangl, with the former wondering what Gangl was going to say or do in response to what he had just told him. Although he could see by his uniform that Gangl was not SS, he would not have necessarily known that he would respond positively to what he had to say. For all Krobot knew, Gangl could have just been listening to what he had to say so that he could then inform an SS unit of what he had learned about Itter Castle.

Gangl wanted to help but he also knew that with just ten men under his command, there were limitations to what he could actually achieve. Any SS unit in the area would have been heavily armed and comprised of considerably more men than he had at his disposal. Consequently, Gangl and his men then headed northeast, in the general direction of where he believed he would eventually come across American forces. Having travelled a distance of about 30 miles they reached the outskirts of the town of Kufstein. Although a relatively short journey, it had been a rather perilous one, because for safety reasons they had driven under the 'protection' of a white flag, which on the one hand would clearly let any American units they might meet know they were not looking for a fight. However, displaying a white flag was also extremely dangerous because if they bumped into an SS unit, the chances were that they would have killed them for even contemplating surrender.

It was in the town square at Kufstein where Gangl and his men, along with Andreas Krobot, met a small American reconnaissance unit under the command of Lieutenant John C. 'Jack' Lee, who was in charge of four Sherman tanks from the 23rd Tank Battalion, 12th Armored Division of the American XXI Corps. Gangl did not, and would never fully appreciate his good fortune that day, as the only reason he actually came across Lee and his men was because they were waiting to be relieved by their colleagues from the 36th Infantry Division.

Gangl quickly explained the situation to Lee, and as had been the situation for Krobot earlier in the day when he had met up with Gangl, Lee had no real idea what he was getting himself and his men into. For all he knew, Gangl could have been lying and simply leading him and his men into a deadly trap. But Lee believed what Gangl had told him, and after contacting his senior officers for their approval, which they granted, Lee, his thirteen men and their four Sherman tanks, along with Gangl and his ten men in their Kubelwagen and truck, began the 40 mile journey back to Itter Castle in an effort to save those being held there. It was a race against time as they had no idea how long it would be before SS units would also arrive at the castle, or if indeed they were there already.

The journey was not without incident. When they were only about 4 miles from the castle, they met a small unit of SS men who were in the process of setting up a roadblock, but after a short exchange of gunfire between the two sides, the combined German and American force won through and continued their journey on to the castle.

Lee, Gangl and their men arrived at Itter Castle later the same day to discover that they had made it there before the SS had, but they knew it was simply a matter of time before they did so. What they did not know was how many men they would be up against and the fire power which they would have at their disposal.

Another aspect to consider here is the extremely difficult decision Lee had to make in relation to even trusting Gangl and his men. Besides being enemies, the two men had never met before, and so Lee had to make a call in relation to whether Gangl was being honest in his intentions. Although clearly dressed in the uniform of a Wehrmacht officer, for all he knew Gangl and his men could have been members of the SS who were simply trying to deceive him so that they could gain entrance into the castle without having to fight their way in. Thankfully, that was not the case, and Lee's decision to trust Gangl proved to be the right one.

The biggest weapon available to those in the castle was Lee's Sherman tank and its rather impressive 30-mm machine gun, which when used in close combat was lethal. In return, the Germans gave as good as they got, but Bochmann, the commander of the 17th SS-Panzergrenadier Division, knew that if he was to have any chance of gaining entry to the castle, his men had to put Lee's Sherman tank out of action, which they eventually managed to do. It must have seemed more like the 4 July celebrations, with the continuous sound of gunfire going off all around the castle. The holes in the castle wall were increasing in number and becoming bigger and bigger.

One can only imagine the depth of mixed emotions the French prisoners must have had when Gangl and Lee arrived at the castle. A feeling of relief and euphoria that Krobot had been successful in finding assistance, but maybe also a slight hint of disappointment in the small numbers of rescuers he had managed to return with. Although they had the benefit of their defensive position being a castle, they knew that no matter how many SS men they came up against, they would be heavily armed and ruthless in their attempts to get inside.

The anticipation felt by those in the castle would have been palpable. A combination of uncertainty, fear and trepidation would have undoubtedly been the order of the day. Knowing an attack was coming, but knowing when exactly that was actually going to be would have been the most difficult aspect to have dealt with, as being on heightened alert for a continuous period of time takes its toll on the strongest of individuals.

On the night of 4 May those in the castle took it in turn to keep a look out for any kind of surprise attack by the SS, as they had no idea when, or from what direction, it would come. Having said that, the SS were limited as to an obvious entry point. If they had sufficient artillery pieces and shells, they could have simply placed their weapons at strategic positions and blasted away, hour after hour, until the castle was nothing more than a smouldering shell of its former self. Although a reasonable tactic to employ, it did not provide absolute certainty that those inside the castle would be killed. The only way this could be achieved beyond all reasonable doubt was to fight their way in and engage those whom they encountered. The latter of the two options was fraught with danger and likely meant they would sustain heavy casualties in the process.

It would have been a restless night for all concerned within the walls of the castle and not many of them would have had much in the way of sleep. There were some minor exchanges of gunfire between the two sides intermittently throughout the night, but it is believed this was more about keeping the castle's defenders 'on their toes' and trying to gauge their numbers and weaponry strength for the real fight, which would take place in earnest later that day.

Lee had placed his Sherman tank, which he had named *Besotten Jenny*, immediately in front of the castle's main gates, although its powerful M3 75-mm machine gun was not a piece of equipment anybody would want to be on the receiving end of. This was more of a defensive manoeuvre designed to prevent the SS from even thinking about making a full-frontal assault on the castle. The M61 round which the M3 fired could punch its way through 3.5 inches of armour at 1,000 yards, so understanding what it could do to the human body would not be that hard to imagine.

Having amassed what they deemed sufficient numbers of men to be able to affectively assault the castle, the

SS began their attack at dawn on the morning of 5 May, which at that time of the year would have been around 4 o'clock. Early in the fight, Lee's tank was taken out by an artillery shell fired from a German 88-mm artillery gun, which was just as effective and feared when being used as either an anti-aircraft or an anti-tank weapon. Thankfully, none of Lee's men was killed or injured when *Besotten Jenny* was put out of action. Corporal Szymcyk was actually in the tank at the time it was struck, but remarkably he survived, managing to jump clear from Lee's pride and joy just before it was hit by a German artillery shell.

The numbers of SS men involved in the attack is estimated to have been somewhere in the region of 150. The fact that those in the castle held out for as long as they did is truly remarkable. Up against a larger, battle-hardened and much better armed force, the outcome of the fight should have been a forgone conclusion, but the castle's defenders fought with a steely determination to save the lives of the French dignitaries with whom they had joined forces to protect. Only one of them was killed, and that was Gangl, shot whilst bravely saving the life of Reynaud.

During the early stages of the fight, communications between those inside the castle and those at the headquarters of the 36th Infantry Division at Kufstein were lost. Thankfully, it was known by the senior officers in charge of the 36th, that a 'battle' was underway, so they wasted no time in sending out reinforcements to assist their beleaguered colleagues. What had been impossible to do before communications had been lost was for Lee to pass on the enemy's full strength, so that those dispatched to assist them would at least have some idea of what to expect upon their arrival at the castle.

It was because of this predicament that one of the prisoners, Jean Borotra, the famous French tennis star and previous member of the Vichy government, offered to leave the comparative safety of the castle to try to meet up with the Americans, and to pass on this vital information. This would not have been a decision that Borotra's wife, who was with him in the castle, would have been happy about, no matter how well intended it was. It must have been a difficult decision for Lee to have had to make in giving permission to let make Borotra leave the castle. Here he was in the middle of a battle, where every soldier he had at his disposal was extremely valuable, but he also knew that it was just as important to let those making their way to the castle know what they were going to be up against. Once Borotra had made his offer, Lee would have known that regardless of any doubts he might have had about the situation, he had no real choice but to let him go.

For Borotra to leave the castle whilst the fighting was going on was an act of supreme bravery on his part, especially as he had absolutely no idea of the number of attackers who were outside the castle walls waiting for him, or more importantly, where they were. When Lee agreed to this action, he would no doubt have also had to consider the scenario where Borotra was captured by the

SS and interrogated about the numbers of those who were in the castle, the weaponry and amount of ammunition they had at their disposal.

Besides the issue of being up against a stronger force, Lee also had to consider the issue of ammunition. They did not have an exhaustible supply, and if help did not arrive soon, then there was a real risk that they would run out of ammunition and have no other option but to surrender, which for most, if not all of them, would have meant almost certain death. Lee for one was not the type of man who was going to go down without a fight. The one advantage that Lee and those in the castle did have was their elevated position, which meant that any assault on the castle by the SS troops would have to be carried out uphill, making them easy targets.

When later recalling the incident with Borotra, Lee said that 'Jean Borotra was the spark of the defence. He volunteered to jump over the castle wall and make his way to Wörgl to summon help. It meant a run across forty yards of open field before he could reach cover. I refused.' But just half an hour after making that decision, Lee realised that matters were not going as well as he had at first hoped, so he changed his mind and let Borotra leave the castle.

An article which appeared in the 12th Armored's divisional newspaper *Hellcat News*, dated Saturday, 26 May 1945, claimed that Borotra never made it to the advancing armoured vehicles of the 36th Infantry Division, which could be seen in the distance by those inside the castle. Lee claims that he opened fire with a 30-calibre machine gun, sending bursts of fire into woods, but ahead of the approaching American armoured vehicles, to draw their attention to the fact that if they opened fire on the castle, they would be doing so on American forces. Lee claimed that this action prevented his colleagues from attacking the castle with their artillery pieces. Lee's claims do not make any sense, as the 36th Infantry Division's headquarters had specifically sent out reinforcements to help those in the castle. That being the case, why Lee told the *Hellcat* newspaper that story is unclear.

Borotra not only met up with the American forces, but he continued with them all the way to Itter Castle, where they arrived at about 4 o'clock in the afternoon. The sight of the 36th Infantry Division's arrival at the castle undoubtedly had an all-round effect. Whilst morale boosting for the French, German and Americans inside the castle, it must have been a deeply depressing sight for the SS who were outside, trying their best to get in.

Once the American relief forces arrived, it was not long before the battle was over and the remaining SS troops were rounded up, many of them happy to surrender rather than fight to the death as might have been expected of them. The question remains as to how fanatical they were by the time of the battle. The oath sworn by all members of the SS declared that they would be loyal and brave to the Führer and that they would pledge their allegiance to him until their death. The Battle of Itter Castle took place just five days after the death of Adolf Hitler had been announced. Whether news of his passing had reached the ears of the fanatical members of the SS, including those involved in the fighter there, is unclear, but either way, they decided that surrender to the Americans was a better alternative than death.

It is quite remarkable that those in the castle managed to hold out for as long as they did. The fighting raged for approximately nine hours before the men of the 17th SS Panzergrenadier Division finally surrendered. How much longer they would have been able to survive is unclear, but they were running low on ammunition by the time the men from the American 142nd Infantry Regiment arrived to end the fighting.

This battle was most definitely a fight of good against evil. For the Americans to do what they did was quite remarkable, as it was for the Wehrmacht soldiers. For them the war was all but over, and it would have been understandable if they had not become involved and simply stayed in the relative safety of their camp and seen out the final few days of the war, without putting their lives in imminent danger. As for the French dignitaries, they had no other option but to fight, otherwise there was every chance that they would be killed.

The news of Germany's impending surrender would no doubt have been common knowledge, not only amongst American and other Allied forces, but the Germans as well. With that in mind and knowing full well that the war was soon to be over, most involved in the fighting would simply be concerned with staying alive and making sure that they were not killed.

One thing that quite possibly saved the castle from being overrun, besides the bravery and dogged determination of those inside, was Lee's tank, *Besotten Jenny*, which had been placed at the main entrance to the castle. When it was destroyed by a shell fired by an 88-mm gun, it also meant that it could not be moved out of the way, ensuring that the castle's main entrance, the obvious and easiest way in, could not be properly utilised. This was quite possibly the single most important decision made by Lee which saved the castle and those inside from being captured and or killed.

With the fighting over and the castle secured, there was no time for the now liberated French VIPs detained within its walls to sit back, relax and enjoy their sumptuous surroundings, because later the same day, their freedom secured, they were evacuated by the Americans back towards France.

As for the German Wehrmacht soldiers who fought alongside the French prisoners and American soldiers, they became prisoners of war, all accept Major Gangl, who was shot dead during the battle whilst trying to protect the former French Prime Minister Paul Reynaud.

Just two days after the fighting at Itter Castle, the German High Command agreed to the Allies' demand for an unconditional surrender, and in doing so, brought an end to the fighting throughout Europe after nearly six years.

Kurt Siegfried Schrader

Kurt Siegfried Schrader was born in Magdeburg, Germany on 28 August 1916, in the middle of the First World War, when his own father was a soldier serving in the Imperial German Army in France. After the war he returned to his family and his previous life, but he appears to have been one of many former German soldiers who had become disillusioned by the manner in which his country had been defeated. During the 1920s, Hitler and the Nazi Party began their rise to power with promises of making the country great again by returning it to its previous level of importance and influence on the world stage; an approach which clearly impressed Schrader's father and influenced his political thinking.

Being brought up in such a family environment in 1930s Germany would have understandably been a major influence on any young man, and Schrader was no different. Like thousands of other young German boys, he joined the *Hitlerjugend*, or Hitler Youth movement, on 1 May 1930, when he was just 13 years of age. He remained

Itter Castle.

Above left: A guard of the SS-Totenkopfverbande (SS-TV), similar to the guards in place at Itter Castle.

Above right: The main entrance to Dachau concentration camp. Itter Castle was placed under the camp's administration in 1943.

Above left: Édouard Daladier, the former French Prime Minister, was a prisoner at Itter Castle.

Above right: Léon Jouhaux, French union leader and prisoner.

Above left: Paul Reynaud, French politician and lawyer.

Above right: André François-Poncet, former French ambassador to Germany.

Above left: French General Maurice Gamelin.

Above right: Georges Clemenceau, French politician.

Above left: French General Maxime Weygand, another of those held at Itter Castle.

Above right: François de La Rocque, founder of the French Social Party.

Left: Jean Borotra, the French tennis ace.

Below left: Georg Bochmann, the man in charge of the SS units who attacked the castle.

Below right: 88-mm artillery gun, the type used to bombard Itter Castle.

Above left: SS men preparing to fire a Panzerfaust.

Above right: SS soldiers preparing to begin their assault on the castle.

SS with Panzerfausts.

Above left: Josef 'Sepp' Gangl, the German Wehrmacht officer who helped in the defence of Itter Castle.

Above right: Kurt Siegfried Schrader, an SS officer who also helped with the defence.

American soldiers and tanks on their way to Itter Castle.

Above left: German and American troops fought side by side in the battle.

Above right: US officer John Carey 'Jack' Lee (right) and other American officers.

Middle: American soldiers and a tank rush the rescue.

Right: American General McAuliffe leading former French prisoners from the castle.

French
dignitaries
following their
liberation.

Captured
German SS
soldiers.

Itter Castle
showing
damage
by 88-mm
artillery fire.

a member until 7 April 1937, when he joined the German Army, becoming a member of the feared SS the very same day. Because of his ability to speak English, he was initially attached to the SS-Nachrichtensturmbann, or intelligence section, located in Berlin.

On 20 April 1940, he received a commission as an SS-Untersturmführer (Second Lieutenant) and was posted to the SS-Totenkopf Division's Infantry Replacement 2nd Battalion, where he remained until 17 May 1941, at which time he received a further promotion, this time to the rank of SS-Obersturmführer (First Lieutenant) and was transferred as an adjutant to the Begleit-Battalion Reichsführer-SS.

On 1 February 1943, Schrader had been transferred to the 2nd Battalion, 10th SS-Panzergrenadier Division 'Frundsberg', and it was whilst serving with that unit he was promoted to the rank of SS-Haupsturmführer (Captain). Sometime after the Allied forces had landed at Normandy, Schrader was wounded in combat trying as best he could to hold back the advancing Allied armies. Whilst convalescing from his wounds he was attached to his division's Training and Replacement Battalion, with whom he remained until 7 February 1945, after which time he was transferred to the SS-Feldersatz Brigade 102.

On 6 March 1945, Schrader's unit was ordered to re-join the 'Das Reich' Division, who had already been deployed in Hungary, but because of a surprise American attack just two days later, which had captured the river bridge at Remagen, that order was cancelled. Instead, along with every other available unit in the surrounding area, they were dispatched to Remagen and placed under the command of the 11th Panzer Division.

By the time of the battle at Itter Castle, SS-Hauptsturmführer Schrader was convalescing and recovering from wounds in the nearby village of Wörgl. He took the decision to help the French dignitaries who were held at the castle during the battle on 5 May 1945, rather than side with his SS colleagues. His assistance would have been invaluable to the overall defence of the castle as he would have been fully aware of the tactics that would be deployed. It could be said that Schrader's decision was a brave one, because if the SS had managed to breach the castle and win the battle, he would have known that he would have likely been the first defendant to be killed.

It was quite possibly as a result of these actions that he only spent two years in captivity as a POW after the end of the war. The unknown factor here is why an SS officer would suddenly take the decision to help Allied civilian POWs rather than fight alongside his fellow SS colleagues. Was it because he had finally grasped the big lie Hitler and the Nazis Party had spent so long trying to sell to the German people as well as to all his military units? Or was it because he understood that the war was lost, and his priority was now doing everything that he could to stay alive and secure his own safety and security in a post Second World War Europe? Had he, as is often claimed, 'defected' and joined the Austrian Resistance movement, or was it simply a case of doing whatever he needed to do to save his own skin? Going from being a supporter of Hitler and the Nazi Party from the time of his early teens to that of a hard-lined SS officer, to then suddenly changing his mind and becoming an individual with a completely different mindset is not a concept that is so easy to accept without at least questioning it. Having said that, he had been reprimanded for what was classed as 'SS-unworthy conduct' on 18 July 1941, when he was an Obersturmführer with the Begleit-Bataillon Reichsführer-SS. What actions or conduct he had displayed to warrant such a punishment is unknown to the author.

SS-Hauptsturmführer Schrader wrote an unpublished memoir, and although the exact date of when he wrote it is unclear, it was definitely later than 26 November 1961 as he refers to an article which appeared in a German illustrated magazine entitled *Neue Illustrierte*, which was a political weekly publication which was in print between 1946 and 1961.

To obtain a true picture of what a particular individual is truly all about, reading their own description of an event is so much more powerful than an author paraphrasing what they have said. When that individual is an officer, their words hold even more importance because they help provide an insight not only about themself, but how they feel about those they are directly responsible for. What they say shows their real intentions, their personality, their ethics, what is important to them, and what they hold dear to their heart.

What follows is an extract from Schrader's memoir:

The Americans had taken the bridge without a fight at Remagen, the Wehrmacht units were on the run or disbanding. I managed to escape American encirclement and captivity at the last minute with some of the men of my staff. It was after a small rest with my unit, with which I finally returned to Nabburg via Coburg after much exertion. That was not a safe undertaking; for scattered units that had no valid papers with them – my small troop was one of them – if they were apprehended by the so called 'Flying Field Courts of the Führer', they were usually sentenced to death, which was then immediately carried out. We were lucky! But in Nabburg I immediately received a new order to deploy to Hungary in the Budapest area. On the way there, I first contacted the SS headquarters in Vienna. There I learned that it would no longer be possible to continue to the new location in Hungary due to the advance of the Russians. I was advised to report to the SS headquarters in Bad Tolz in order to receive further orders. I drove, I think it was 24 April 1945, shortly after Hitler's birthday, from Vienna to Wörgl near Itter, where my family lived. On the way, our train, which was not a troop transport train, was caught in an aerial attack by an English fighter bomber near Melk in Austria. They shot the locomotive out of action. The passengers left the train in a hurry, for the Jacobs returned again and again and shot at the fleeing ones like in a rabbit hunt. After several hours we were finally able to continue the journey with a replacement locomotive. In the evening I arrived at Itter and was reconciled with my family.

I knew that the front position had got worse and worse but the next day I contacted Lieutenant Colonel Giehl, the commander of the Army Mountain NCO school in Wörgl. I had met this officer, an Austrian, during my military hospital stay in Wörgl. After I had informed him that my marching orders were to Bad Tolz, he told me that this trip was no longer possible since the Americans had already reached Munich. He asked me to take over the function of IB officer on his staff, which was to supply the troops with weapons, vehicles, and food. In the meantime, Lieutenant Colonel Giehl had become combat group commander and thus belonged to the 'Unternehmen Alpen-Festung'. With this company Hitler hoped for another turn of the tide of the war. With his units, Giehl was responsible for the Inn section, such as the Kufstein-Jenbach line. The military situation changed hourly to our disadvantage and in order to avoid further human casualties, we officers in the staff of KG Giehl urged him to give up the fight. He, too, accepted the senseless resistance and agreed to our proposal. He asked me to take his wife and children with him to my family in Itter, because he feared fighting in the Inn Valley near Wörgl.

Schrader was handed a typed letter by Giehl. It contained the following:

> SS-Hstuf Schrader, placed himself at my disposal on 28 April 1945 to the service in my staff. Hstuf. Schrader, who due to his wounds is no longer suitable for an active combat role, was released by me on 2 May 1945, from my staff to his hometown of Itter.
>
> In the absence of an official seal, dated 2 May 1945, Giehl, Lieutenant Colonel Commander.

Schrader arrived back at his home with Frau Schrader and her children later the same evening. Once safely indoors and knowing that the war for him was over, he removed his uniform, which in every sense was a more than welcome weight off his shoulders. It was at this time he learnt Wimmer, who had previously been in touch with him, seeking permission to leave his post at Itter Castle because of the imminent arrival of American forces, had taken his men and left.

Returning to Schrader's memoir:

> On 5 May 1945, the 'Red-White-Red' station in Innsbruck issued an appeal which was then repeated several times, with the following wording.
>
> 'Attention! The former French government was interned at Schloss Itter. The population is asked to take care of the imprisoned.'

It is not immediately clear what the 'Red-White-Red' station was, but it was quite possibly an official Allied marking scheme to distinguish each other from enemy forces. The same colours were most definitely added to Allied vehicles during the Second World War.

The next part of Schrader's memoir is particularly interesting, especially about Léon Jouhaux having visited Schrader at his home:

Innsbruck had shortly before been occupied by the Americans, who had advanced there from Italy. Shortly after this special report, Mme Brüchlin and Léon Jouhaux came to see me in my apartment; they had also heard the report, as had all the detainees, and asked me, but as quickly as possible, to the castle, which was about 200 m away from my apartment, to come. The French who knew me, wanted to talk with me. I went there immediately and found almost all the French gathered in the courtyard of the castle. Michel Clemenceau was the spokesman and spoke to me in German and asked me as a German officer to take care of the security of the French internees until the arrival of the Americans. Since there were only a few guards left, I pointed out that it could be very difficult to defend against attacks by German troops retreating to Kitzbuhel. I could act as a negotiator in the event of an attack. I finally agreed, only asking for permission to bring my wife and two children into the castle. This wish was immediately granted, and I went to Itter.

The fact that one of those who had approached Schrader for his help had been the French Trade Union leader Léon Jouhaux, had not been widely reported. Nor the fact that Schrader had taken his wife and two young children into the castle with him. Either way it would have been a difficult decision. If the castle had been taken by the SS, it is more than conceivable that all those inside would have been killed, but if he had left his family at home and the SS had discovered their identity, the outcome would have more than likely been the same.

Schrader's very presence in Wörgl could be described as brave, if not somewhat risky, as the town was not known for its Nazi sympathies. In fact, many of the local population were against National Socialism, and as an officer in the SS, Schrader epitomised everything they stood against politically. Some of the townsfolk had even been sent to Theresienstadt and Ravensbrück concentration camps, where they subsequently perished, because of their anti-Nazi views.

Schrader's memoir continues the story:

On the way I met a German Kubelwagen which stopped immediately. In the car were Major Gangl, a man from Stuttgart whom I still knew from KG Giehl, and Rupert Hagleitner, who was in civilian clothes and wore a red and white armband. He was the leader of the resistance group in the Wörgl area. With them was an American officer, Lieutenant Lee from the 36th Infantry Division (Texas Division). I told Major Gangl, who had joined the resistance movement with some soldiers of his German unit, that I had taken over the security of the French prisoners and asked for military protection. On the spur of the moment Hagleitner had led the two officers to Itter; the whole area was still in German hands. But the three officers left the castle again to seek military protection. When I returned with my family shortly afterwards, the French women had made a tricolour and attached it to the castle tower next to a white flag. Both flags were visible from afar.

When I told the French about my meeting with the American officer, everyone hoped, albeit with mixed feelings, for a good ending. After about 1 to 2 hours an American Sherman tank with about twelve American soldiers came back to the castle. Likewise, Rupert Hagleitner had appeared again.

I gathered the French now and officially handed them over to the American officer. My mission was fulfilled, but Lieutenant Lee asked me to stay at the castle until further reinforcements would come, as he still feared German attacks. So, I spent the night with my family in the castle. The next day was 5 May, and we walked early in the morning, in wonderful weather, in the castle courtyard. The American tank stood about 50 m away from the castle and was clearly visible from the valley side. Between 8-9 o'clock an attack of German units, which were on the retreat from Wörgl in the direction of Kitzbuhel, began against the castle, because Wörgl had been occupied by the Americans at night. The Germans were units of the Waffen-SS. Flak rounds struck the castle turret, and my wife, who threw herself over our children in a protective manner, was slightly injured by falling stones. The Sherman tank received a direct hit and burnt out immediately.

The Waffen-SS units Schrader refers to here were the ones under the command of SS-Oberführer (Colonel) Georg Bochmann, the man in charge of the 17th SS-Panzergrenadier Division 'Götz von Berlichingen'. Bochmann was in some ways a bit of a contradiction. At Itter Castle he was more than comfortable with attacking it, knowing full well that it was mainly fully of elderly French civilians and non-combatant individuals, rather than carrying on his way through Bavaria, yet when he was ordered to carry out an attack on advancing American forces by Generalfeldmarschall (Field Marshal) Ferdinand Schörner, the Commander-in-Chief of the German Army High Command, he refused, believing the orders were suicidal. This refusal resulted in Bochmann being sacked by Schörner, and if it had not been for the state of the war at that time, he would have undoubtedly faced a court martial, which could have ultimately resulted in his death.

Schrader's memoir continues:

The soldiers, Americans, and German together, shortly afterwards fought off an attack, during which Major Gangl fell. Even some of the French internees took part in the defense. For security reasons, the remaining persons gathered in the castle cellar. All feared the worst. Since there was no connection to the outside world, the well-known tennis player Borotra, his age at the time was about 45-50 years, tried to get from the castle to Wörgl on foot in order to get American help. I myself observed the military situation with Lieutenant Lee from the castle tower. Around noon we recognized American tanks on the valley road from Wörgl in the direction of Kitzbuhel, which slowly advanced because there was still German resistance. About 2 o'clock, five to eight tanks came to Itter with an American Colonel; the Germans had withdrawn.

Borotra, who had managed to get through to Wörgl, also came back with the Americans. He was accompanied by the Yugoslav concentration camp prisoner, Cichkowitz, who immediately jumped at me and shouted something like, 'Well, Hauptsturmführer'. He looked at me with rage, as if he wanted to kill me, but cook Andra intervened and explained that I had stood up for the French with my life. I introduced myself to the American Colonel and again handed the French over to the Americans.

It is believed that the individual who Schrader's refers to as Cichkowitz is the same person who in other references to the Battle of Itter Castle is also known as Zvonimir Čučković, and the man he calls Andra, is the Czechoslovakian, Andreas Krobot.

The man Schrader refers to as 'the American Colonel', who he handed the French prisoners over to, is clearly Colonel George Lynch, the commanding officer of the 142nd Infantry Regiment.

Schrader continued:

He thanked me for my service, and the liberated French were told that they should prepare to travel and be taken by plane from Innsbruck to France. Before I left the castle with my family, I received a letter of thanks from the French; it was written by Mrs Bruchleu [Augustine Brüchlen], with the following content in French.

'SS-Hauptsturmfuhrer Kurt Siegfried Schrader took over on 4.5.45, the security of the French internees in castle Itter. He remained with them during the German attacks.'

This important document was signed by all the former French prisoners.

It is unclear, and somewhat confusing, to try to understand why Schrader believed those few lines written by Augustine Brüchlen, who at the time was the mistress of Léon Jouhaux, constituted being such an important document. It included no kind of 'thank you', nor did it make any mention of his personal actions or heroic deeds he had carried out whilst he was at the castle. However, the fact it was signed by all the French prisoners potentially shows that he intended to use it as a 'guarantor' in case he was captured by the Allies, and to use it as proof that he had helped French civilians in case he should subsequently be charged with any wartime offences. After he left the castle, Schrader, his wife, and children returned to his apartment in Wörgl. In completing his memoire, he gave himself a big pat on the back by commenting on how the occupants of his village, in particular the village's catholic clergyman, who he named as Höck, congratulated him on his service to the French. Why they would feel the need to do that is somewhat of a mystery.

Part of the article about Schrader which appeared in the *Neue Illustrierte* magazine in 1961 appears to have included a comment made by one of the castle's prisoners at the time of the battle, former French Prime Minister Édouard Daladier. Because of the manner in which Schrader commented about the article in his memoir, it appears to say that Daladier suggested that he (Schrader) had not acted of his own volition, but under orders from Berlin. Interestingly enough, Schrader does not confirm or deny Daladier's comments, but instead said the following:

> The statement of Daladier mentioned therein whether I had orders from Berlin or not, does not apply. Since I had little outside contact, I had to make my own decisions. The responsibility was not easy, and yet I gladly accepted it, I simply had to do it. I was happy about the outcome if you can put it that way.

It could also simply be the case that Schrader had a difficult decision to make about his own personal safety and that of his family. As an SS officer living at home with his wife and children, regardless of whether he had been wounded in action, if discovered by his SS colleagues and unable to convince them of his personal circumstances and with no officially stamped documentation to prove his claim, he faced almost certain execution. If he openly sided with them, he was intelligent enough to understand that if an attack on the castle was successful and those inside were killed, he would be arrested when the fighting finally came to an end. Maybe that is why he ultimately chose to help those being held at the castle. For him and his family it was certainly the better option. The war was over, Germany had lost, and Schrader knew that he had to look to the future, and to have been seen to have openly assisted the Allies by helping to ensure the safety of some very high-powered

French dignitaries was certainly not going to do him, or his family, any harm at all.

Schrader's experience as a soldier and as a member of the SS would have been invaluable to the defence of Itter Castle. When the initial attack began in the early hours of 5 May, he would have known full well that it was not actually a serious attempt at breaching the walls of the castle, but more an attempt at gauging the extent of the castle's defences. He would have also known that once this had been achieved, it would only be a matter of time before the SS would begin their full-scale attack on the castle with a much larger force that would not be so easy to defend against. If Lee had not already worked this out for himself, Schrader would have undoubtedly told him. Time was the important factor. Schrader and Lee would have both known that American forces were on their way to help save their colleagues, along with the French dignitaries, and the SS would have also known this, meaning that their assault on the castle would need to be sooner rather than later.

CHAPTER SIX

Lieutenant John Carey 'Jack' Lee

John Carey 'Jack' Lee Jr. was born on 12 March 1918, in Omaha, Nebraska, an area of the United States well known for its violent thunderstorms and tornadoes, occurring as they do primarily during spring and summer, but also sometimes in the autumn months as well.

The family home was at 155 East Main Street, Norwich, Chenango, and his next of kin was his father, also John Carey Lee, a local doctor by profession. The 1940 United States Federal Census for the home address also shows his mother, Mae Agnes Lee, his two younger brothers, William who was 20, David, who was just 13 and his sister Mary, who was 15.

Prior to becoming a soldier, Carey Jr. had been a second-year student at Norwich University, but on 16 October 1940, at the age of 22, he enlisted in the United States Army at Northfield, Washington, Vermont. On the back of his draft card he was described as being 5 feet 10 inches tall, 190 lbs in weight, with hazel eyes, brown hair, and of a ruddy complexion. Under the heading of

'Other obvious physical characteristics that will aid in identification', was the following entry: 'LEFT EAR – CAULIFLOWER.' No doubt something he picked up as the result of some kind of sporting involvement. As a young man growing up in pre-war America, Lee was a more than competent sportsman, excelling in a number of sports at both high school and university, particularly American football, which went hand in hand with his somewhat brash demeanour.

It was quite possibly his decision to attend Norwich University in Vermont in 1938 which led him to the point in time that would see him involved in the events at Itter Castle in May 1945.

Founded in 1819, Norwich University was respected not just for its students' academic achievements, but it also had, and still has to this day, a renowned military college. Like many of his fellow students, Lee was quick to enrol in the campus' cavalry unit, which was part of the Reserve Officers Training Corps, and soon became adapt at both horsemanship and swordsmanship. Soon after graduating as a Second Lieutenant in May 1942, he was called up and quickly found himself at Fort Knox, Kentucky, having been assigned to the Armored Force School. He took to the three-month course like a duck to water. Such was his grasp of the requirements of armoured warfare, he finished the course with a natural instinct of what to do in any given situation, rather than having a raft of skills that he had been taught by his instructors.

After finishing his time at Fort Knox, Lee was posted to the 12th Armored Division, who at the time were stationed at Fort Campbell in Kentucky. The pace of the war was picking up day by day. By November 1943 the 12th Armored had moved to Camp Barkeley in Abilene, Texas and Lee had been promoted to the substantive rank of First Lieutenant and put in charge of 1st Platoon, Company B, 23rd Tank Battalion. Lee and his men had been provided with Mk 4 Sherman tanks that were fitted with 75-mm cannon, along with 3-mm, and 50-calibre machine guns, making them a formidable fighting force by any stretch of the imagination.

It would be nearly another year before Lee eventually found himself on European soil, as a platoon commander in charge of five Sherman tanks. Having embarked from New York on board the converted passenger Ocean liner the *Australian Empress* in the middle of September 1944, Lee and his men were more than happy to arrive in Southampton some days later, and once again set foot back on dry land.

By November 1944, Nazi Germany was in full retreat, under attack from Soviet forces in the east, along with British, French, and American forces coming at her from the west. But the Germans were certainly not giving up without a fight. The Maginot Line was a formidable defensive structure, consisting of a number of concrete fortifications, anti-tank obstacles, armoured cloches, retractable turrets, artillery pieces, and anti-tank guns, all built by the French over a ten-year period between

1928 and 1938. It stretched from its northern most point, at Charleville-Mézières in Belgium, and continued south, stretching the entire length of the borders which separated France, Italy, Luxembourg, and Germany, before finally coming to a stop at Basel, Switzerland. Its purpose was quite simply to deter a German invasion of France, which had been envisaged for many years throughout the late 1920s and early 1930s, as tensions continued to increase amongst the European nations.

The Maginot Line failed in its purpose when in May 1940, German forces advanced into France by quicky advancing through Belgium, the Netherlands, Luxembourg, and the Ardennes Forest, and in doing so avoided the need of having to undertake a full-on assault on the heavily defended Maginot Line. The newly appointed Supreme Commander of French Military Forces, Maxime Weygand, signed the surrender document with Germany on 22 June 1940 at Compiègne, and with it, all remaining French soldiers laid down their weapons to spend the rest of the war as POWs, including those who had been holding out in different segments of the Maginot Line.

Having arrived in France in November 1944, it was the following month when Lee and his small platoon took part in fighting along the Maginot Line, in particular around the areas of Metz and northern Alsace, to attempt to dislodge the remnants of German forces who were trying their hardest to prevent the inevitable American advance into the Fatherland.

By December 1944, the US 12th Armored Division, which included Lee and his Sherman tanks, were part of the US XV Corps, which came under the command of Major General Wade Haislip. As Christmas fast approached that year, there was no real need, or desire, to send any units on what were seen as unnecessary patrols. Despite the rumours which circulated amongst the American forces concerning the possibility of German attacks, nothing of any real significance actually took place. But despite this, nothing was left to chance. To ensure American safety, roadblocks were put in place, passwords were changed regularly, soldiers were placed on sentry duties at regular distances, and were frequently replaced to ensure that levels of concentration and observations were kept at the highest possible state.

In readiness for the beginning of Operation *Nordwind*, Adolf Hitler delivered a speech to his divisional commanders on 28 December 1944 at his military command bunker complex at Langenhain-Ziegenberg, more commonly referred to as the 'Eagle's Nest'. He declared that 'This attack has a very clear objective, namely the destruction of the enemy forces. There is not a matter of prestige involved here. It is a matter of destroying and exterminating the enemy forces wherever we find them.'

On 30 December 1944, Lee, his men, and the rest of the 12th Armored Division were rotated out of front-line action and placed in reserve. The opportunity to be able to enjoy a much-needed rest was most welcome, but it was to become short lived, as the following day

Germany launched Operation *Nordwind*; its final major offensive of the Second World War. The main objective was to break through the American lines of the Seventh Army, along with those held by the French 1st Army, causing utter confusion in the process, with the ultimate goal being the capture of Strasbourg by 30 January. If this operation proved to be successful, not only would it delay the Allied advance into Germany, but it would also provide their scientists with the much-needed time to develop their *Wunderwaffe* or 'Wonder Weapons' such as the V-2 rocket and H.IX V3 flying wing, with the hope and belief that it would ultimately change the course of the war in Germany's favour.

Initially the German operation met with limited success, but much of that was because of the element of surprise which it had caused amongst American forces. The 12th Armored Division, including Lee and his platoon, were re-assigned to the US VI Corps, who had no reserve units, and were under the command of Major General Edward Hale 'Ted' Brooks. On 8 January 1945, armoured elements of VI Corps, which included Lee and his platoon, were ordered to attack the town of Herrlisheim. American forces eventually entered the town the following day after some fierce fighting, some of which was hand to hand, and house to house. After having nervously cleared a number of houses, the American forces had come up against little in the way of resistance, until they were confronted with German tanks; a commodity which the American's had none of themselves on their own side of the Zorn River.

The 12th Armored Division was thrown into the affray on 16 January, where they found themselves up against German units, namely the 553rd Volksgrenadier Regiment, the 35th, 119th and 2nd Panzergrenadier regiments, along with the 10th SS Division. Lee's unit lost a number of their tanks, so fierce was the fighting. Herrlisheim was finally taken by the Americans on 31 January, but it had come at a price in both men and equipment. The 12th Armored Division had suffered 1,250 casualties and lost 70 of their vehicles. There were two other interesting aspects about the fighting at Herrlisheim. Firstly, Lee and Gangl were both involved in it, and both men received military awards for the parts they played. So impressed were Lee's commanding officers with his efforts during the Battle of Herrlisheim, that he was also promoted. His new rank and position saw him in a reconnaissance role, scouting ahead of the main 12th Armored Division as it advanced into Austria, to ensure there were no unpleasant surprises waiting for them in the form of ambushes or roadblocks. They were also tasked with securing any bridges that were located along the route.

The announcement of Hitler's death at the end of April 1945, besides being met with a hearty cheer by all Allied forces, brought with it not only an enhanced feeling of euphoria, but a realisation that the war would not continue for too much longer. For combatants on either side, the most important thing had become to ensure that they stayed alive. This meant not taking any unnecessary risks, doing only what you had to do, and nothing more.

By the time of the battle at Itter Castle, Lee and his men had not seen much in the way of a break since arriving at Le Harve, France, on 11 November 1944. Just 3 miles after having crossed the border into Austria, they found themselves on the south side of the Inn River, on the immediate outskirts of the village of Kufstein. Other than a German roadblock, which had been put in place on the main road leading into the village, Lee's men had not encountered too much in the way of resistance. On reaching the centre of the village, they came to a halt and had a much-needed break, but even whilst relaxing, they still had to stay alert just in case there were snipers or die-hard SS present who still wanted to continue the fight.

Although he did not know it at the time, just as he was starting to think about the joys of returning to his family back home, Lee would soon be thrust into one of the war's unlikeliest and strangest battles. About 15 miles south of Kufstein, and unbeknown to Lee, the Croatian resistance fighter Čučković had left Itter Castle in an attempt to locate the advancing American forces. Instead, he had stumbled into a group of Wehmarcht soldiers under the command of Major Josef Gangl, who, realising the war was nearly over, was doing his best to keep his men alive and out of danger. Once Čučković had told him about the castle and its occupants, Gangl and his twenty or so men started making their way towards Kufstein. On arriving there they were taken to the 23rd Tank Battalion's commanding officer, to whom Gangl reported the story he had been told by Čučković. The decision was taken to travel to the castle to save those inside.

Lee, as befitted his nature and personality, volunteered to undertake the operation to travel to Itter Castle and liberate those who were incarcerated there. He had given his Sherman tank the nickname of *Besotten Jenny*. His crew with him in the tank were Sergeant William T. Rushford, Corporal Edward J. Szymcyk, Corporal Edward J. Steiner, and Private First Class Herbert G. McHaley. The other tank that went with him was *Boche Buster* and was under the command of Lieutenant Harry Basse. His crew consisted of Technical Sergeant William E. Elliot and Sergeant Glenn E. Shermann. Sat on top of the tanks were a number of men from D Company, 17th Armored Infantry Battalion, whilst men and tanks from the 36th Infantry Division's 142nd Infantry Regiment were also part of the convoy. Major Josef Gangl and a group of his men brought up the rear.

Fortune was to be on Lee's side during the trip to Itter, which was potentially an extremely dangerous journey. Numerous Waffen-SS units were in the area, who had still not given up the fight, and Lee knew that every step of the way he and his men had to focus and concentrate on the job at hand. The first location they came to was the Austrian city of Wörgl, which was only about 10 miles from Itter. Luckily for Lee and his men, the SS unit which had been in the city had left just a few hours before the Americans had arrived, something which they could not have known. What they did find was a number of Austrian partisans.

It was at Wörgl that Lee's convoy began to drastically diminish in size, having agreed to leave five tanks from the 36th Infantry Division behind to help protect the city just in case SS elements should return.

To reach Itter from Wörgl, Lee and his remaining men had to cross a small river which was passable by a bridge. The SS had placed demolition charges on the bridge in preparation for when they felt the need to blow it up. After having the explosives removed, he took the decision to leave *Boche Buster* and a number of men to secure the bridge. Lieutenant Basse, the commander of the tank, did not want to miss out on the action which lay ahead, and instead climbed on board Lee's tank, leaving his in the capable hands of its crew.

Whatever ideas Lee had on what to do next were greatly reduced when it became clear that he did not have enough vehicles to take all his men, Gangl's men and rescue the French dignitaries held at the castle. The only choice he realistically had was to wait it out until help came in the form of advancing American forces. The castle provided as solid a defensive base as was possible, and unless the SS started blowing massive holes through the walls of the castle, then they were as safe as they could possibly be.

On the night of 4 May both sides tested each other with small arms fire, which included a number of the French dignitaries who wanted to be part of the fight, regardless of what their 'position' in French society was, but all of that changed the following morning when the SS unit fired two 88-mm shells towards the castle. The first one hit a room in the upper levels of the castle, and the second round struck Lee's *Besotten Jenny* tank, which he had positioned in front of the castle's main entrance.

Unbeknown to Lee and the others in the castle, help was on its way. Major John Kramers had made his way from Innsbruck in company with Eric Luten, American war correspondent Meyer Levin, and French photographer, Éric Schwab. Men from the 2nd Battalion, 142nd Infantry Regiment, under the command of Lieutenant Colonel Marvin J. Coyle, had also arrived at the bridge that was being guarded by the *Boche Buster* and her remaining crew. Before all setting off for Itter Castle, Kramers attempted to reach Lee over the radio, but to no avail. But, after a moment's thought, he jumped back into his jeep and sped back the short distance to Wörgl, entered the town hall building and simply telephoned the castle direct. Luckily for Kramers, the telephone lines were still intact and he spoke to Lee directly, informing him that help was on the way and would be with them shortly. Kramers then rushed back to his jeep and made haste back to the bridge, but by the time he arrived there the *Boche Buster* and the armoured vehicles of the 142nd Infantry Regiment had already left.

Unbeknown to the Waffen-SS, the castle's defenders were rapidly running out of ammunition, but time was precious for both those inside and outside the castle, albeit for totally opposite reasons. Looking back on these events, the obvious question which immediately comes to mind is why the SS forces did not continue to bombard the castle with its deadly 88-mm gun. If they had continued to do so it would have been an extremely short battle with a totally different outcome. It appears that they only fired it twice, and one of those rounds struck Lee's Sherman tank, the *Besotten Jenny*. If they had continued firing their 88-mm gun, then the attack would have been over much quicker, and those inside would have had the unenviable decision to make as to whether to fight to the death or surrender and hope they would survive.

Despite this unexplained oversight, the SS certainly were showing no signs of giving up. Sometime around 3 o'clock in the afternoon, by which time the battle had been going on for around nine hours, a number of SS men made their way round the remnants of the burnt out *Besotten Jenny* and were preparing to fire an anti-tank rocket into the castle's enormous wooden main gates. Before they could do so, however, the cavalry arrived to save the day in the form of 2nd Battalion, 142nd Infantry Regiment, along with the *Boche Buster* and Major Kramers in his jeep.

Looking back on these events, it is quite incredible that the SS soldiers took so long in deciding they were going to use an anti-tank rocket to gain entrance into the castle. It is as if they were waiting for something. If that is actually the case, what they were waiting for is unclear.

With the fighting over with, and the French dignitaries safely on their way to Paris in a number of hastily commandeered local civilian vehicles, life for Lee, his men and the Wehrmacht soldiers who had fought so bravely alongside them, returned to what it had been like beforehand. Together the American and German soldiers climbed into the back of a large military truck and began the short journey to Kufstein. Once there, the American and German soldiers smiled at each other, shook hands, and went their separate ways. For Lee and his men, it was a well-deserved rest, a shower, and some food, while for the German soldiers it was the beginning of their time spent as POWs.

For his actions leading up to and including the Battle of Itter Castle, Lee was awarded the Distinguished Service Cross, which is only second behind the Congressional Medal of Honor in awards for combat valour issued by the US Army. The citation for his award read as follows:

For extraordinary heroism in action, as Commanding Officer of Company B, 23rd Tank Battalion, in the vicinity of Worgl, Austria, and the Itter Castle on 4-5 May, 1945. Captain Lee with a small group of soldiers infiltrated into hostile territory, demoralised enemy forces, prevented the destruction of two key bridges, and caused 200 German soldiers to surrender. He found many prominent French prisoners at Itter Castle, and immediately organised a defence with both American and German troops. Despite a fanatical SS attack and heavy artillery barrage, Captain Lee's men held until friendly troops arrived. Captain Lee's initiative, boldness, courage, resourcefulness and outstanding qualities of leadership exemplify the highest traditions of the Army and the United States.

Lieutenant Harry J. Basse, who was in command of the *Boche Buster*, was awarded the Silver Star for his involvement in the Battle of Itter Castle.

CHAPTER SEVEN

Wehrmacht Officer Major Josef 'Sepp' Gangl

Major Josef Gangl, a member of the German Wehrmacht, would have probably been nothing more than a minor footnote in the history of the Second World War had it not been for the part he played in the Battle of Itter Castle. Instead, he ended up a hero.

Gangl was born in Obertraubling, Bavaria, in 1910. On 1 November 1928, soon after his eighteenth birthday, he enlisted in Artillery Regiment No. 7 of the German Army. By 1935, Gangl was a married man living in Ludwigsburg and a serving member of Germany's 25th Artillery Regiment. In 1938, Gangl was promoted to the rank of Oberfeldwebel (Sergeant).

At the outbreak of the Second World War, Gangl was stationed in the Saar-Palatinate region of Germany, close to the border with France. It was there that he experienced combat for the first time, as French forces pushed their way across the border. He was wounded during the subsequent fighting and spent the following weeks and months recovering and recuperating in a number of different military hospitals, before finally returning to his unit in May 1940, just in time to take part in the Battle of France, where he was in command of a Wehrmacht reconnaissance unit of the German 25th Infantry Division. After France had been defeated, Gangl spent the following year in a training capacity serving as an artillery instructor. His next posting could not have been more different, as the tranquillity and relatively slower pace of a training environment was replaced by the horrors of serving on the Eastern Front as part of the 25th Motorized Artillery Regiment during the fighting for the Ukrainian capital of Kiev.

During the following eight months, Gangl was awarded the Iron Cross, both 1st and 2nd Class, and was promoted to the rank of First Lieutenant. He remained stationed on the Eastern Front as a commander of a unit in the 25th Artillery Regiment, before returning to Germany in January 1944 to command an artillery replacement and training department, located at Höchstädt an der Donau, Bavaria.

By the time the Allies landed at Normandy in June 1944, Gangl was serving with the Werfer-Regiment 83, who soon after the initial landings had been ordered to make their way to the French city of Caen, where they came under the command of the 12th SS Panzer Division 'Hitlerjungend'. On 11 June 1944, in the area close to Carpiquet airfield, they defended the city against the attacking Canadian soldiers. After having sustained heavy losses, Gangl and his comrades in Werfer-Regiment 83 were fortunate enough to escape from the Falaise Pocket in August 1944, the fighting for which had resulted in an estimated 10,000 German dead and a further 50,000 who were captured by the Allies.

As part of Werfer-Brigade 7, Gangl took part in the famous Battle of the Bulge from December 1944 to January 1945, followed by an ever-quickening retreat towards Germany. It was becoming increasingly clear that the war had become a lost cause and that it was just a matter of time before defeat became a reality.

Gangl, a proud and brave German soldier, had more than done his bit to serve his country the best he could. He had led from the front, setting an example to his men. On 8 March 1945, he had received the German Cross in Gold, which is awarded for repeated acts of bravery or military leadership. He was further promoted to the rank of Major and placed in command of the 2nd Division, Werfer-Regiment 83, with orders for him and the remainder of his men to make their way to the Tyrol Valley for the defence of what was referred to by the Germans as the Alpine Fortress. On arriving there he was sent to the Austrian city of Wörgl by the commander of the XIX Mountain Corps, Lieutenant General Georg Ritter von Hengl, who assigned him to the Giehl Kampfgruppe (Combat Group), commanded by Lieutenant Colonel Johann Giehl.

Giehl had given Gangl specific orders to defend Wörgl by blowing up bridges and to barricade roads in an attempt to slow the advancing American forces, and to fight to the last man. That was the initial plan, but von Hengl changed his mind after elements of the Giehl Kampfgruppe were attacked by the 12th US Armored Division on 3 May 1945 in Niederaudorf, Bavaria, and suffered heavy losses. In response, and possibly with the knowledge that the end of the war was nigh, von Hengl decided it was time to withdraw his remaining troops from both Wörgl and Itter.

This was the time for Gangl to show his true colours. He disobeyed Giehl's orders to blow up bridges and raise barricades in Wörgl, along with von Hengl's order to withdraw from the town and that of nearby Itter. This was extremely brave of Gangl for two reasons. Firstly, his actions should, and could, have resulted in him being executed, and they would have if either Giehl or von Hengl had got their hands on him. Secondly, he did not know how his men would react to his decision to blatantly disobey his orders. There was also a third problem in the shape of the Waffen-SS, who had moved into Wörgl and Itter after von Hengl had ordered the withdrawal of his troops.

Gangl was clearly an intelligent, brave, caring, and thoughtful individual, because not only did he disobey von Hengl's direct order, but he also liaised with the Austrian Resistance in the area who were under the command of their leader, Alois Mayr. Making such contact had its own dangers as there is no way Gangl could have known exactly how it would unfold. Mayr could have understandably believed Gangl was doing no more than trying to lead him into a trap, and killed him, but despite the obvious risks to himself and his men, Gangl still took the risk because he knew that morally, it was the right thing to do.

The situation Gangl found himself in was complicated even further. Most of the German military, along with the civilian populations of Wörgl and Itter, knew that the war was all but over, and that it would not be long before Allied soldiers were in the area. To try to reduce any confusion about what kind of reception the American soldiers would receive, the townsfolk had taken to hanging white flags from their windows. This was an understandable action, but also both brave and dangerous at the same time, because Heinrich Himmler, the man in overall charge of the SS, had ordered that any home caught making such a display was to be entered and all male residents inside were to be shot. Preventing this from happening was one of the main reasons Gangl remained behind in Wörgl, albeit with only ten of his men.

It was an interesting gesture by Gangl, who even in a time of war still had the trait of humanity. He did what he did because he knew it was morally the right thing to do. As a soldier and an officer, he knew that it was his moral duty to protect civilians from acts of tyranny, no matter which side the aggressors were on.

The unanswered question about Gangl is why did he disobey Giehl's orders? Was it because he was a God-fearing man who, late in the war, had recognised the error of his ways and wanted to make amends for the despicable regime he had fought so valiantly for? Or was it because he knew the war was a lost cause and wanted to acquire as preferable surrender terms as was possible for him and his men? Whichever it was there is no questioning his bravery as he stood shoulder to shoulder alongside American forces and the castle's prisoners in the fight against an SS unit who were determined to break into the castle and kill all of those inside, including Gangl and his men. Although the SS never broke in, Gangl did not leave the castle alive after becoming the victim of a well-aimed SS sniper's bullet.

In summer 1945, one of Gangl's men, Lieutenant Erich Blechschmidt, wrote his wartime memoirs entitled *The Last Days: War Diary of 'Unit Gangl'*. The memoir included his comments and observations about the events at Itter Castle, and beforehand at the nearby town of Wörgl. Much of the memoir was translated into English and included in a blog by Clarissa Schnabel, and some of its content is included here with her kind permission.

Although this book is ultimately about the Battle of Itter Castle, Wörgl plays a significant part in the overall story as it is where Gangl met the Croation resistance fighter Zvonimir Čučković, who had left the castle looking for help to rescue the French dignitaries being held there.

It is also clear from what Blechschmidt says that he and the rest of the men from the unit held Major Gangl in very high esteem. Blechschmidt mentions two occasions when just days from the end of the war, Gangl was given orders by General Staff Officer Lieutenant Colonel Karl-Heinz Knospe, both of which he refused to undertake.

The first order was to send two detachments of men to Günzburg and rescue men of the 13th Waffen-SS Division and lead them back to the comparative safety of the Augsburg bridgehead. Gangl only changed his mind when he was threatened by Knospe with being shot by a firing squad, but even then he managed to get the better of his commanding officer. He duly sent out two detachments of men as he was instructed to do so, but not to Günzburg, but towards Munich instead. Soon after this, Knospe, apparently none the wiser that Gangl had actually disobeyed his order, then instructed him and his men to mount an attack on the American forces located across the River Lech. Once again Gangl refused to carry out the order, even though on this occasion Knospe threatened to shoot him with his pistol. This was in keeping with Gangl's overall wartime motto, 'Das Leben ist ein Würfelspiel' (life is a game of dice). Indeed, Gangl even went so far as to make a die the symbol of his former unit, Werfer-Batterie LIII.

An entry in Blechscmidt's memoir for 27 April 1945 describes the local population's feelings towards the SS:

We are located in Götting near Rosenheim. The population is very bitter! After all, an SS unit murdered the pastor and the teacher of the village by shooting them in the back of the neck yesterday. These bandits who had been quartered in Götting since January were not idolised by the population but were treated as people of the same blood, and as thanks for their hospitality they could not refrain from murdering the priest and the teacher when they left. That is once again so typical of the SS! The elite of Germany, as they call themselves.

It was soon after this that Gangl took command of the remaining remnants of the regiment, after Knospe and his staff had done a disappearing act having been in fear for their own personnel safety.

Gangl, Blechschmidt, and the remainder of their unit arrived in Wörgl, having decided to make their way there from Götting, where their intention was to wait until they were able to surrender to the advancing American forces.

Wörgl had become a magnate for the remnants of a number of Wehrmacht units, but more worryingly for the local population there was the large number of SS men still in town, who were not quite so welcome. As previously discussed, some residents in Wörgl and the surrounding towns and villages had hung white flags from the windows of their homes to let advancing American troops know that they were welcome. To the SS this was simply an excuse to enter these properties and kill all male occupants they came across.

Blechschmidt explains how it was in Wörgl where Gangl met up with local resistance fighter Alois Mayr. It was to him that he offered his help, and that of his small band of men from Regiment 83, by protecting the local population from the threat posed by the SS units still in the area. Initially there would have undoubtedly been trepidation and uncertainty on Mayr's part as to whether he could trust Gangl, or whether he was simply looking to lead him into a trap. The fact that Gangl had remained in Wörgl would have ultimately been enough proof for Mayr that he could be trusted, as he would have seen that all the other Wehrmacht units had already left town.

Alois and Gangl discussed what they believed was their best course of action. From this it was agreed that the blowing up of bridges and roads in and around Wörgl, an instruction which had been ordered by Lieutenant Colonel Giehl, would not be carried out, and that collectively they would do what they could do to help the French dignitaries being held at Itter Castle.

Gangl knew that despite his military uniform and rank, his life was potentially in danger if he came into contact with members of the SS. After all, if they were not convinced of his authenticity and loyalty to Hitler and the Nazi Party, they would more than likely have shot him on the spot. To this end Blechschmidt explained how Giehl's order to defend Wörgl against the advancing American forces was used by Gangl and his men to move between Wörgl and Landl, where they set up a signals post. What Gangl did not know was that Mayr had managed to find out that the Nazis had 63 tons of explosives stored at Kufstein to be used to carry out his orders to defend the town and blow up the roads and bridges.

On Wednesday, 2 May 1945, with the Battle of Itter Castle just a few days away, a meeting took place in Wörgl. Those present included Lieutenant Colonel Giehl, Major

Gangl, and two of his officers, Captain Dietrich and Lieutenant Blechschmidt. Giehl proceeded to provide detailed information about the fighting to come, oblivious to the fact that Gangl and his men had already changed their allegiance to that of the Austrian Resistance.

Blechschmidt's notes are extremely useful as they help paint a more rounded picture of what happened at both Itter Castle, and in Wörgl, the day before and after the French dignitaries were liberated.

In the morning of 4 May, one of Gangl's men, Sergeant Künzel, handed over a number of weapons and ammunition to members of the resistance in Wörgl, which included a man by the name of Rupert Hagleitner, and three others who are only known by their surnames of Pitzinger, Blattl and Zangeri. The main purpose of this was so that Wörgl and the meagre food supplies it had left could be protected against those in the area who were tempted to try to take them for their own needs.

The resistance group already had a cache of weapons hidden in the Neue Post Inn in Wörgl, with the knowledge and co-operation of the landlady, Frau Lenk. The cache was discovered during a routine search by members of the SS whilst Blechschmidt and Mayr were having a conversation nearby. Local resistance fighters who were at the inn before the search of the premises took place managed to escape just in time and were not discovered. Somewhat surprisingly, nobody was executed by way of a reprisal for the discovery of the weapons, although the SS officer leading the search was, it is reported, extremely angry.

Wörgl had a large food warehouse which would have no doubt been an attraction for tired and hungry retreating German troops making their way through the town. At about 4.30 pm on Friday, 4 May, a German artillery battery arrived in Wörgl under the command of Lieutenant Möckel. In no time at all men from his unit attempted to loot the food warehouse. An armed confrontation quickly ensued which resulted in Mayr, Blechschmidt, and two Wehrmacht soldiers, privates Zeiher and Eckstein, managing to safeguard the warehouse and its contents. Möckel's men eventually backed off before any shots from either side were discharged.

Blechschmidt explains that whilst events were unfolding at Wörgl, an important meeting took place at Kufstein between Major Gangl and the Americans Colonel Lynch and Captain Lee. The discussion centred around the protection and liberation of the French dignitaries at Itter Castle and the Americans' willingness to assist in a joint venture with Gangl and his men. Although Lee was clearly up for the challenge, Colonel Lynch had his concerns as to whether or not he could entirely trust Gangl and his men, so much so that he told Gangl he would hold him personally responsible for Captain Lee's safety. In response Gangl gave Colonel Lynch his word of honour that he was completely trustworthy, and that Lee was in absolutely no danger from him or any of his men.

Gangl and Lee then set off for Wörgl and on route they passed a number of German units who were still to be found in some of the villages they passed though. On each occasion a conversation took place between Lee, Gangl and the officer in charge of each of the units, and every one of them, on the strength of just their word, was trusted to lay down their arms and not to take part in anymore fighting against advancing American forces. At each location, Lee and Gangl ensured that any German explosives which had been put in place were removed before they continued their journey. There was one exception to this when the Wehrmacht soldiers who were guarding the bridge at Gratten refused to either leave the area or to lay down their arms. To ensure the bridge was not blown up and destroyed, one of Gangl's men, Lieutenant Schmidt, remained behind. It is hard to believe that Schmidt on his own would have posed enough of a deterrent to prevent those at the bridge from blowing it up if they had chosen to do so.

At about 5 o'clock the same day, a meeting took place at the office of Alois Mayr in Wörgl, which included Lee, Gangl, Hagleitner, and Pitzinger. This was the first time that Gangl and Hagleitner had actually met each other. Hagleitner introduced himself as being the leader of the Austrian Resistance in Wörgl, whilst Lee informed Hagleitner and Pitzinger that he could be back in Wörgl with his tanks in less than two hours.

Blechschmidt explained it was whilst this meeting was taking place that Andreas Krobot, one of the prisoners being held at Itter Castle, suddenly arrived at Mayr's office in Wörgl and inadvertently interrupted the meeting with a note from the French dignitaries, written in English, asking for help. The time for talking was clearly over.

Major Gangl, having promised his men that he would safely get them through to the end of the war unscathed, asked for volunteers to join him and Lieutenant Blechschmidt in their efforts to protect the French prisoners. The following men stepped forward: sergeants Kliment and Weiske, corporals Zeiher, Lehman, Fischer, Haude, Eckstein, and private Happel. These men, accompanied by the American officer Lee, Hagleitner, and another member of the local resistance, set off on their mission.

Lee, Gangl, and his men, along with Hapleitner and his colleague, arrived at the castle just before 6 o'clock in the evening, where they were met by Édouard Daladier and the other French dignitaries. The greeting was somewhat of a mixed reaction because although they were happy that help had finally arrived, they were clearly expecting a more substantial number of men to protect them from the onslaught they feared would follow.

Gangl's men who had remained behind, along with other Wehrmacht units still in Wörgl, had all been placed under the command of Alois Mayr. It was a difficult situation which Gangl found himself in. On the one hand he wanted to keep his men safe and alive so close to the end of the war, whilst at the same time he wanted to protect the civilian population in Wörgl and liberate the French dignitaries. It truly was a 'juggling act' of epic proportions.

Blechschmidt explained how at about 8 o'clock on the evening of Friday, 4 May, and despite the obvious danger, he and Private Zeiher left the castle on a scouting mission to see if they could find the exact location and number of SS units nearby, but their whereabouts were not discovered. The rest of the evening was relatively quiet and uneventful, but those in the castle remained on high alert as they awaited the inevitable attack.

The first exchange between the two sides took place early in the morning of Saturday, 5 May, but this was not the beginning of a full-scale attack. Blechschmidt was not alone in realising it was nothing more than an attempt by the SS at trying to gauge the numbers of defenders in the castle, along with discovering what type of weaponry they had at their disposal.

According to Blechschmidt's account of the events, when the SS first fired their 88-mm artillery into the castle, Major Gangl remained calmness personified and was actually having a bath. He did this knowing full well that an attack by the SS was imminent. While there is no reason to suppose Blechschmidt was lying, it still seems a very strange thing for Gangl to have decided to do, knowing the events that were about to take place.

When describing the outbreak of the battle, Blechschmidt poignantly observed in his memoir: 'Machine guns bark their hot, bloody sun on both sides. Hand grenades detonate! We are again in the middle of the bloody craft of war. But one thing we know, it is for the last, one way or another.'

He goes on to explain that Gangl was shot sometime around noon as the sun was high in the sky. The shock of

Gangl's demise clearly affected the German soldiers who saw him lying motionless on the ground to such an extent that Lee had to shout at them to keep firing.

. Blechschmidt, in almost poetic prose, describes their collective feelings: 'There lies our Major, our friend and comrade of many years. Our father!'

At about 1 o'clock in the afternoon he could see men and tanks of the American 142nd Infantry Regiment advancing towards the castle from the direction of Wörgl, which signalled the beginning of the end for the SS still involved in the attack.

The excitement of the Americans and German defenders at the castle was tempered by the realisation that in their attempts at preventing the SS from continuing their assault, the shelling by the quickly advancing 142nd was getting closer and closer to the castle, too close in fact. To let the Americans know that the castle had not been overrun, Blechschmidt explained that a tricolour was quickly located and hoisted aloft the castle. In referring to the men of the American 142nd Infantry Regiment, he makes the comment, 'our friends are attacking'.

With the fighting over and their work done, the American and German soldiers shook hands and shared a smile, before collectively saluting the dead body of Major Gangl. Blechschmidt described how the journey back towards Wörgl, with the body of Major Gangl, was more like a funeral march than one of victory for him and the rest of the German soldiers, before finally laying his body down in the town's chapel.

The irony of the situation was that Gangl had promised his men he would get them safely through to the end of the war, a promise he was unable to see through for himself.

In reference to Gangl's funeral, which took place in Wörgl on Wednesday, 9 May 1945, Blechschmidt said the following:

A wonderful pre-summer day makes Tyrol glow. But this sun is not shining for us today, our hearts are sad and empty. This afternoon with the entire population of Wörgl attending, we entrusted what was mortal in our commander to the quiet, calm earth of Tyrol. He has returned home to his mountains. Many words were spoken, but we who knew him, remained silent. A few furtive tears, a wistful reminiscence of the past days together with him, that was our thanks.

We have seen the bloody harvest of death, comrades and friends taken from us. No one thought it would also take our father from us.

The final paragraph in particular emphasises the high esteem in which all Gangl's men held him. In fact, it was not just his comrades who felt this way. In the post-war years, the residents of Wörgl offered to build a home in the town for Gangl's wife and her son, Norbert. This offer came about due to Nazi sympathisers in Ludwigsburg,

Gangl's hometown, making accusations against him for disobeying orders, helping the Austrian Resistance, and fighting against, and killing, members of the SS during the fighting at Itter Castle.

I could find no better way of finishing this chapter other than to include the following letter written to Gangl's wife. Although the author of the letter is unknown, the manner and style in which it is written hints that it was penned by Gangl's loyal friend and fellow officer, Lieutenant Blechschmidt.

I am shocked to hold the card from the Ludwigsburg Residents' Registration Office in my hands, which tells me that your husband was killed in action in Wörgl/Tyrol on 5 May 1945. It is more than tragic that it had to be in the last five days. He, who led our 'bunch' with great skills and a sure hand through many a merciless and fierce enterprise. At that time, we were the fire brigade of the 53rd Army Corps and were deployed at focal points. I joined this unit in May 1942 as a lance corporal, became a non-commissioned officer with Herr Gangl, and received the Iron Cross, 2nd and 1st Class from him. In the Bobruisk area, our boss pinned his own Iron Cross 1st Class on my chest, as only a certificate arrived for me from the army corps. From this small gesture you can see what a fine comrade he was. He was an officer, but first and foremost, he was a comrade.

CHAPTER EIGHT

Oberführer Georg Bochmann and the 17th SS Panzergrenadier Division 'Götz von Berlichingen'

The battle-hardened men of the 17th SS Panzergrenadier Division 'Götz von Berlichingen' were kept at bay for just over nine hours by a combination of a group of disillusioned German Wehrmacht soldiers, a number of French dignitaries, both civilian and military, and American soldiers, not to mention others who were being held as prisoners at Itter Castle. It was a truly remarkable achievement which took place in extremely unusual circumstances.

The 17th SS Panzergrendier Division was a unit of the Waffen-SS, formed in October 1943, in the French city of Poitiers, on the River Clain in central France, and was made up of Romanian Germans along with French and Italian volunteers.

The division was given the honour title of 'Götz von Berlichingen', which was a reference to a fifteenth-century

German knight who lost his right hand in battle, but who subsequently had it replaced with a prosthetic one made of iron, hence why the division's emblem was a clenched iron fist.

At the time of the Battle of Itter Castle, the man in command of the 17th SS Panzergrenadier Division was SS-Oberführer (Captain) Georg Bochmann, a holder of the Knights Cross of the Iron Cross with Oak Leaves and Swords, which was the highest German military award of the Second World War.

Bochmann joined the Nazi Party in 1933 and became a member of the SS the following year when he was posted to the newly opened Dachau concentration camp on the outskirts of Munich. Its initial purpose was to hold individuals who were opponents of Hitler and the Nazi Party, but during the course of the war this changed to include Jews, criminals and foreign nationals from German occupied countries. But Dachau was not just one camp, and by the time the main camp was liberated on 29 April 1945 by advancing American forces, there were somewhere in the region of 100 sub-camps, with Itter Castle also coming under its command. Such was the brutality of the regime at Dachau that 32,979 deaths were recorded as having taken place there, although it is more than likely that many more perished. The largest number of deaths at the camp took place during the six months leading up to its liberation, many of which were never documented.

Overall conditions in the camp deteriorated dramatically over the course of the ten months leading up to its liberation, with malnutrition, sanitation, and disease (mainly Typhus), out of control. This was hardly surprising when the number of inmates increased from 20,000 in August 1944 to more than 60,000 by April 1945.

Ironically, after their capture at Itter Castle, Bochmann and his men would find themselves being held at the same Dachau camp they had previously commanded.

Bochmann was an experienced soldier and leader who had begun the war with the rank of Obersturmführer (First Lieutenant) and was one of those involved with the creation of the Totenkopf division of the SS. Whilst in command of an SS-Totenkopf unit he saw action at Cambrai, Arras and at Dunkirk during the Allied evacuation in May and June 1940. It was because of his efforts during the French campaign that he was awarded the Iron Cross, 2nd Class, promoted to the rank of Hauptsturmführer, and put in charge of the 3rd SS Division Totenkopf, who remained in France until they were sent to the Eastern Front to take part in Operation *Barbarossa*, the invasion of the Soviet Union in the spring of 1941. Whilst fighting on the Eastern Front in Kaunas, Lithuania and Dunaburg in Latvia, Bochmann was awarded the Iron Cross, 1st Class.

Bochmann and his men had little in the way of respite from the fighting, and by February of the following year they were still fighting on the Eastern Front, having to deal with the severe cold of a Russian winter. They were involved in the savage fighting at Demyansk, just south of Leningrad, which saw 100,000 German soldiers encircled by the Red Army for more than three months. They were so tightly surrounded the only way they could be supplied with food, clothing and ammunition was via air drops by the Luftwaffe. For his actions during this time, Bochmann was awarded both the Knights Cross and the Demyansk Shield, which was awarded to German Army personnel who had served in the area for a minimum of sixty days.

Still on the Eastern Front, Bochmann was further promoted to the rank of Sturmbannführer (Major) in April 1942 whilst still serving with the 3rd SS Division Totenkopf, this time as the commander of the 2nd Motorised Battalion. After two and a half years of sometimes savage fighting, Bochmann and his men were sent back to France for maintenance purposes on their vehicles, and some well-deserved rest and recuperation. For most men, serving and surviving on the Eastern Front for so long whilst enduring the harshness of battle and the extreme Russian winters would have been more than enough, but Bochmann was not so lucky. Maybe it was because of the quality of his leadership or his reputation as a man who got the job done, in early 1943 he returned to the Eastern Front, this time as the commander of the 3rd Motorised Battalion. In February and March 1943 he was involved in the Battle of Kharkov, which resulted in a German victory, and him being awarded the Oak Leaves to his Knights Cross, given to an individual for outstanding leadership, distinguished service, or personal gallantry.

Bochmann was certainly different to a lot of his contemporaries. He was well-respected by his fellow officers as well as the men under his command. If he was not receiving a military award, he was being promoted and transferred to another unit. He was a man whose reputation saw him repeatedly involved in some of the war's toughest fighting, and he did not once shirk his responsibilities.

Bochmann also saw action as the commander of the 3rd SS Division's panzer regiment at the Battle of Kursk, which lasted for more than a month between 5 July and 23 August 1943.

The problem with fighting a war on two opposing fronts is that men, munitions, food, and equipment can sometimes become stretched very quickly, and quite often when it is least expected. This is exactly the predicament that Hitler's soldiers found themselves in between July and August 1943. Just four days after the Battle of Kursk began, 160,000 British, American, Indian, Canadian, Free French, and Australian forces came ashore on the beaches of Sicily as part of Operation *Husky*.

German troops who were undergoing training in France and who were ear-marked for either deployment to the Eastern Front, or as reserve forces for the same front, were instead hastily sent to Italy to help support their colleagues who now unexpectedly found themselves up against an extremely large Allied invading force. Realising the seriousness of the predicament he was now in if Allied forces managed to gain a substantial foot hold in Italy, Hitler had no alternative but to pull his troops out of the Soviet Union and transport them more than

2,300 miles from Kursk towards Sicily. The Battle of Kursk turned out to be the last strategic offensive Hitler was able to launch on the Eastern Front against Soviet forces.

Having been involved in the fighting at Kursk, Bochmann and his men of the SS Panzer Regiment also took part in the fighting along the Mius Front in the Donbas region of the Soviet Union and Ukraine. The Mius Front was a German defensive line created by German forces back in October 1941. In some places it was more than 10 miles in depth, making it a formidable defensive position for any attacking army to attempt to circumnavigate safely. It included mine fields, concrete bunkers, pillboxes, machine gun positions, barbed wire, tank traps, trenches along with artillery positions, which could be moved from one location to another within the defensive line. The Russians finally made their way through it in August 1943 during their Donbas Strategic Offensive.

Bochmann's actions and leadership throughout this fighting earned him another promotion to Obersturmbannführer (Lieutenant Colonel) on 9 November 1943. He was wounded during the fighting along the Mius Front and was sent back to Germany for medical treatment and to recuperate, the latter of which he would have no doubt been eternally grateful for. Whilst enjoying the break from the fighting and the constant reminder of his own infallibility due to the constant involvement in the death and destruction of war, he was first and foremost a fighting man, so his next position must have come as somewhat of a shock to him. He was made head of the SS Officer School for at Arolsen, Hesse, in central Germany.

November 1944 was a busy time for Bochmann. He was further promoted to the rank of Standartenführer (Colonel) and found himself serving with the 2nd SS Panzer Division 'Das Reich', whose reputation as a battle-hardened unit was only matched by the wanton brutality its men displayed during their involvement in the massacres of 643 civilians at the French village of Oradour-sur-Glane, and in the town of Tulle, where 117 civilians were murdered and 149 sent to Dachau, where 101 of them subsequently died.

No sooner had Bochmann been posted to the 2nd SS Panzer Division 'Das Reich', than just eleven days later, he was moved on, this time as the commander of the Armoured Regiment of the 9th SS Panzer Division 'Hohenstaufen'. Although only formed in 1943, the different units of the division saw active service on both the Eastern and Western fronts, including at Normandy, Arnhem and during the Ardennes Offensive.

In January 1945, Bochmann was on the move again when he was put in charge of 18th SS Volunteer Panzergrenadier Division 'Horst Wessel'. Formed in 1944, it was part of the 1st SS Infantry Division and was made up of a large number of ethnic Germans from Hungary. Bochmann would see action with his new unit on both the Western and Eastern fronts. Whilst fighting against Soviet forces at Oberglogau in Silesia (now Głogówek, Poland), the division suffered heavy losses and came close to being entirely surrounded. During the sometimes-savage fighting, Bochmann was wounded, but despite his injuries he continued to command his men and even managed to break out of the ensuing encirclement and lead his men to safety. For his actions at Oberglogau, Bochmann was awarded the Swords to his Knights Cross, Oak Leaves, and the prestigious Wound Badge in Gold. Just ten days before Hitler's reported death, Bochmann was further promoted to the rank of Oberführer.

In mid-April 1945 Bochmann received his final posting of the war when he was put in command of the 17th SS Panzergrenadier Division 'Götz von Berlichingen'. It was at this time he went against his previously loyal record when he blatantly disobeyed orders given to him by Generalfeldmarschall Ferdinand Schörner when he refused to carry out attacks on Allied forces that he saw as being both futile and somewhat suicidal, at a time when he most surely knew it would not be long before Germany officially lost the war and would have no option but to surrender. In response, Schörner stripped Bochmann of his command, although by that time of the war his words held little, or no weight at all. The war was a matter of days from its finale and for most German soldiers they only had two things in mind; to stay alive and to be captured by the Americans and not Soviet forces.

It would be interesting to know what motivation the men of the 17th SS Panzergrenadier Division had for such an action as the one they undertook at Itter Castle. For them there was absolutely nothing to be gained. If they had been successful in their attack, it would have simply resulted in more members of the SS facing charges of war crimes after the end of the war. These were, after all, fanatical young men who believed in the Nazi cause as if it were a religion or a prescribed way of life, one which they were wholeheartedly committed to without question, and one that many of them were prepared to die for if necessary.

Despite refusing to attack American forces and having been relieved of his command, on 5 May 1945 Bochmann still led his men in the attack. One must wonder what he would have done with those inside if he had been successful in taking the castle. Despite several of his men being killed and more than 100 taken as prisoners of war, Bochmann managed to escape after the event. Four days later, having made his way back to Germany, he surrendered to American forces in Rottach-Egern, some 23 miles from Itter.

Georg Bochmann was not charged with any crimes for his wartime involvement and saw out his days in the German city of Offenbach am Main, in Hesse, where he died on 8 June 1973 at the age of 59.

CHAPTER NINE

US 36th Division's *T-Patch News* and the 12th Armored Division's *Hellcat News*

During the Second World War many Allied units produced periodical newsletters or newspapers that were printed for the consumption of its officers and men with specific news about what individual units had achieved, although what information appeared in each of the publications had to be approved first as there was no desire for the men's morale to be negatively affected. After all, the main reason for these news feeds was to maintain and keep up morale.

The US 36th Division and the US 12th Armored Division both had such newsletters. The 36th's version was the *T-Patch News*, whilst the 12th had the *Hellcat News*.

Volume 4, No. 1 of the *T-Patch News* was dated 8 May 1945 and marked up as a 'Special Edition' because it included news that the war was over and that the Allies had won after Germany had agreed to an unconditional surrender.

The following is an article which appeared on the front page of this edition of the newspaper and describes the events at Itter Castle:

Internationally Prominent French Group Liberated by Four 142nd Infantrymen

After two years of captivity in an Austrian castle, a prominent French group, Premiers Daladier and Reynaud, Generals Weygand and Gamelin, the sister of General De Gaulle, and Borotra, noted tennis star, were rescued by four infantrymen of the 36th Division.

The four men were from Easy Company, 142nd Infantry. They had been sent forward by Lt.Col. Marvin Coyle, their battalion commander, who had been offered the castle in surrender by the German major of the garrison there.

Riding a tank, the four doughboys reached the castle in the early evening, accepted the major's surrender, and stayed there while waiting for the rest of the battalion to come up.

On the following morning they were attacked by desperate SS troops attempting to retake the castle and perhaps kill their former prisoners. The four men stood them off for a while. Then the tank in the castle gate was knocked out.

The German major armed his men to aid the 142nd men in holding off the SS troops who were trying to storm the castle. The German major was killed during the defense.

At 1500 hours the next afternoon the battalion drove through the SS ranks and opened the road to the castle for good.

The four infantrymen who seized the castle, who were all reinforcements in their first major action, were: Pvt. Al Worsham, Louisville, Ky.; Pvt. Alex Petrunkowich, Chicago, Ill.; Pvt. Arthur Pollock, Pottstown, Pa.; Corp. William Sutton, Superior, Wis.

Paris has since announced that Borotra and Weygand have been placed under arrest.

While an interesting read, it is not necessarily a wholly factual account. The article appears to suggest that the four men of Easy Company, 142nd Infantry, had single handily beaten off the SS unit and saved the day. Maybe the article was simply trying to galvanise morale amongst its men at the end of the war? Perhaps it was nothing more radical than a piece of harmless self-effacing propaganda? Either way it had conveniently omitted the part played by the Wehrmacht soldiers and the men of the 23rd Tank Battalion, not forgetting the part played by the French tennis star, Jean Borotra, and the castle's handyman, Zvonimir Čučković.

The second edition of the 12th Armored Division's newspaper, *Hellcat News*, was printed some two weeks after the end of the war, in Heidenheim, Germany, and was dated Saturday, 26 May 1945. It featured articles about the division's many recent achievements, including one written by Corporal John G. Myer, of B Company, 23rd Tank Battalion, which told the story of the unit's involvement in the Battle of Itter Castle.

12th Men Free French Big-Wigs
By Corporal John G. Mayer, Company B,
23rd Tank Battalion.

American troops, soldiers of the Wehrmacht, and a handful of French personages slated for death by the SS, fought side by side in an alpine castle on the last day of the war in Bavaria.

Among the 14 French notables rescued by the tankers of the 12th Armored Division were former Premier Édouard Daladier, along with aging General Maxime Weygand, who commanded the French armies when the Germans broke through into France. The French tennis star, Jean Borotra, and his wife, as well as a sister of the present chief executive of France, General Charles de Gaulle.

Also, in the strangely mixed pro-and-anti-Nazi group were a former French labor union leader and Michel Clemenceau, son of the World War I statesman.

Top heroes of the scenario-scrap were Lieutenant John C. Lee, Junior, commanding officer of Company "B" of the 23rd Tank Battalion, and his gunner, Corporal Edward J. Szymcyk.

Across the Border

Their saga began on the afternoon of May 4 shortly after their platoon took Kufstein, just across the Austrian border, after knifing through a well-defended roadblock. Into the town came a German major, under a flag of truce, who said that he was in position to surrender a large force of enemy troops and 14 notables, once connected with the pre-Pétain governments of France.

All, he said, were at a castle in Litter [*sic*], eight kilometres away. Lee and Szymcyk immediately left with the major but when they arrived, the German colonel in command refused to surrender.

Back in Kufstein, Lee picked up his reinforcements, two tanks from his own outfit and five more from the 36th Infantry Division's 142nd Battalion. With Lee and Szymcyk went Lieutenant Harry Basse, from Santa Ana, California, a maintenance officer, and the tanks' crews. At the town of Wörgl the force paused. Lee, leaving the others behind, took his own medium tank with five volunteers, said goodbye to his rear-guard, and rumbled on to the castle, the faithful major trailing in his car.

Then began the classic defense of the ancient 'schloss', which had not known battle since the days of crossbow and boiling oil. The defenders numbered 41 in total, there were 20 soldiers of the Wehrmacht (German regular army), 14 French men and women, and seven Americans.

At 4 o'clock on the morning of May 5, a small force of SS men launched an attack up the slope toward the castle. American rifles and German light machine guns teamed up to beat them back.

Tennis Star Helps

'Jean Borotra was the spark of the defence,' Lee recalls. 'He volunteered to jump over the castle wall and make his way to Wörgl to summon help. It meant a run across forty yards of open field before he could reach cover. I refused.'

But half an hour later things started looking tougher, so Lee permitted Borotra, whose name ranks among the immortals of tennis history, to make what was a brave but futile dash. Soon after he left, tanks of the 36th Infantry Division were sighted in the distance.

Guessing that they hadn't received Borotra's message and instead regarded the castle as simply another German stronghold to be blasted out of the way, Lee and Weygand quickly teamed up on an American 30-calibre machine gun and opened fire sending long bursts crackling into the woods well ahead of the approaching tanks.

'It worked,' Lee said. 'Later I found that the tankers had their heavy guns trained on the castle ready to fire when they recognized the sound of the American "thirty" and decided it was a signal rather than a threat.'

So, the possibility of being killed by their own rescuers was averted for Lee and his men, who included, in addition to those already named, Technical Sergeant William E. Elliott, Corporal Edward J. Seiner, and Private First-Class Herbert G. McHaley, Linton RFD 1, Ind.

Sergeant Glenn E. Shermann of Cameron, Mo., served as both the radioman and gunner on Elliot's tank. Private Joseph Wall, from Selma, North Carolina, was left to guard the bridge alone all night, armed only with a carbine, but still he managed to capture a number of German prisoners. The SS, however, had no compunctions about blasting away at the castle. Their 88 mm shells crashed through the thick outer walls of the ancient castle, landing in several of its rooms, and wounding one of the German soldiers who had become one of its defenders.

Last Fight on Front

At 3 o'clock on the afternoon of the 5th, the cautiously advancing tanks of the relief force, led by Elliott and Sherman, after 16 hours pounded through the opposition, and arrived at the castle like mechanized cowboys in a new-style Western movie. Lee's saga was ended. His tank, 'Besotten Jenny,' as she was fondly dubbed by the Negro troops, was kaput. All the infantry peeps were filled with notables. So, Lee and his heroes climbed onto a truck loaded with German prisoners and rode ingloriously back to their outfit. They arrived just in time to hear the radio broadcast that all German troops in the south had agreed to stop shooting that day at noon. Theirs had been the last fighting on the whole southern front. But there's a postscript: a few days later Lee's promotion to Captain was announced and his men have all been cited for decorations.

After five months of almost non-stop involvement in the war Lee and his men were physically tired, but the main thing which kept them going was the knowledge that the war's end was as close as it could possibly be. Lee cared deeply for his men and the last thing he wanted was for any of them was to lose their lives. He wanted them to survive the war and return home safely to their families. As he waited patiently, if not a little nervously at Kufstein, he wished for nothing more exciting than for the war to be over. But after speaking with Gangl, this was not to be the case.

CHAPTER TEN

'Prominente' - Prisoners in the News

Although it was only French dignitaries who the Nazis had held captive at Itter Castle during the actual battle, after the fighting was over, British and American prisoners who the Nazis believed had a similar value to them in potential future negotiations with the Allied authorities were brought there, with the castle acting almost as a type of clearing station for those liberated dignitaries who had been held captive at other nearby locations in the Tyrol area of Austria.

These were all men who had served in either the American or British armed forces during the course of the war and had been captured at different locations throughout Europe. Once their identities had been discovered and their significance had been recognised by the Germans, their future potential value was realised. With this in mind, they were separated from those they were captured with and eventually ended up in locations throughout the Tyrol.

The names of these important individuals often appeared in the British Press and included Lord Lascelles, a nephew of King George VI. A captain in the 3rd Battalion, Grenadier Guards, he had fought at Monte Corno in Italy where he was wounded and captured on 18 June 1944. Many years after the war, Lascelles said the following about his wartime incarceration.

> We thought it was absolutely ridiculous. There were about half a dozen of us with well-known connections and we were of absolutely no importance ourselves. We were all, let's call it, relatively junior officers from [aged] 30 something downwards. Our fear was that someone would rumble that the bargaining power was a great deal less than they'd first thought it was, that they'd calculate one way and then it turned out another, and then we'd become expendable. That was our fear. Once the Wehrmacht, the army, lost interest in us, we were frightened of becoming prisoners of the Gestapo or something like this, which would have become very disagreeable. We just avoided it. We spent the last night of our time not at Colditz, but actually in Austria by then, where the guns of the guards were pointing outwards at the Gestapo, who might come in rather than us who might have tried to get out.

Lascelles words are quite prophetic and show that his position and that of his compatriots was very similar to that of their French counterparts held at Itter Castle. In fact, unbeknown to Lascelles, Adolf Hitler had signed his death warrant in March 1945, but SS-Obergruppenführer Gottlob, who was chief of all Germanys prisoner of war camps, as well as being in charge of German forces in the Bavarian Alps, including units of the Waffen-SS, refused to carry out the order. This was quite possibly because, knowing the war was close to an end, his focus was suddenly on saving his own life and he knew that he had more to lose by killing Lascelles than he did to gain.

Lieutenant Felix Malcolm De Hamel, a cousin of Prime Minister, Winston Churchill, whose nephew, Giles Romilly, a civilian journalist with the *Daily Express* newspaper, was also one of those in German custody after being captured during the commando raid on the Norwegian town of Narvik in May 1940. Romilly was the first such prisoner to be classified by the Germans as a *Prominente*, an individual who was regarded by Adolf Hitler as to having great value due to their connection to prominent Allied figures.

A number of British *Prominente* officers were held at Colditz Castle, but as the war approached its end many of them were moved towards safer locations in Austria with some of them staying overnight at Itter Castle on their way to freedom and whilst waiting to begin their journeys back to the UK.

An interesting aspect about the Battle of Itter Castle is that whilst researching it, I discovered that other than in newspaper articles there is very little mention about the British individuals held captive there. The main reason for this is that most of the British POWs only arrived at Itter Castle during early May 1945 or after the battle took place, having been moved there from other camps located throughout Germany as the country was gradually overrun by advancing Allied forces. By way of example, it was known that Viscount Lascelles had previously been held at Colditz Castle in Saxony Germany, which was liberated by the Americans in April 1945. Any time he may have spent at Itter Castle would have only been a fleeting one after he had been liberated from Colditz and then simply moved 'back down the Allied lines' to safety, rather than having been held there as a prisoner of war.

The fact that these individuals were being moved to 'safer locations' as late as the middle of April 1945 shows that Nazi Germany still believed they had value, and that when the inevitable time came for them to surrender, they could be used as bargaining chips to achieve certain advantageous terms and conditions.

Stories about several prominent POWs appeared in the British press throughout the war. In June 1944, the *Birmingham Daily Post* ran a story about Lord Lascelles' capture in Italy:

Lord Lascelles
Nephew of the King
A Prisoner
Wounded in Italy

The following statement was issued last night from Harewood House: -

Lord Harewood has had official intimation that Lieutenant Viscount Lascelles is reported wounded and missing and believed to be a prisoner of war.

Lord Lascelles is twenty-one. He is a nephew of the King and elder son of Lord Harewood and the Princess Royal. Before joining the Army, he worked at the Harrogate headquarters of the West Riding War Agricultural Committee.

Lord Lascelles is an officer in the Grenadier Guards, his father's old regiment, of which Princess Elizabeth is Colonel-in-Chief. He joined the Grenadiers as a private when he was nineteen. In November 1942, he was gazetted second lieutenant. He was in the Home Guard before joining his regiment.

German radio claimed last night that Viscount Lascelles had been captured on the Italian front. The announcer said: 'The enemy has built on both sides of Lake Trasimene a focal point from where he intends to thrust with concentrated forces at the Arezzo cross-roads. Here are the enemy's *elite* troops, mainly infantry, tanks, and artillery, among them the British 6th Tank Division from which we captured Lieutenant Viscount Lascelles, a nephew of the King of England, some days ago.'

A Canadian broadcast from Italy last night said: 'Viscount Lascelles was wounded near a town which was later taken by the Eighth Army. His condition was such that he could not be moved except by a jeep, which a comrade volunteered to obtain. On returning he found that Lord Lascelles and his men were missing.'

Later in the war, an article appeared in the *Bradford Observer* of Monday, 7 May 1945 with the headline 'Harewood Village Rejoices – US Troops Freed Viscount Lascelles'. The end of the article is of particular interest here because it references the events that had taken place at Itter Castle:

Lieutenant Viscount Lascelles, Grenadier Guards, son of the Princess Royal and Earl of Harewood, was among a group of notable prisoners released by the Germans to the United States Seventh Army.

After being wounded last June Viscount Lascelles was taken prisoner in Italy.

There was great joy and relief when the news of Viscount Lascelles' release became known. News of this was conveyed to Lord Harewood by the

Press Association, and official confirmation was received later.

'We are delighted to hear the news,' said Lord Harewood's secretary, and similar expressions of joy were made to a 'Yorkshire Observer' reporter by a member of the household staff last evening.

Viscount Lascelles' release was also a major topic of conversation at the Harewood Arms, the licensed hotel in the village, the landlord, Mr. Storey, saying the news had come 'as a great relief' to the village, 'for things had not looked too good for the Viscount before.'

As there is yet, no knowledge of the date on which Viscount Lascelles is expected home, Mr. Storey said that no special celebrations had yet been arranged by the villagers, but that there was a big likelihood of something being done when the date became known.

Queen's Nephew Free

Also released is Captain the Master of Elphinstone, nephew of the Queen.

Captain Elphinstone, of the Black Watch, was taken prisoner in 1940.

Others released were Lieutenant John Winant, son of the United States Ambassador to Great Britain. Lieutenant Michael Alexander, a relative of Field-Marshal Alexander, and Lieutenant Felix Malcolm Dehamel, a relative of Mr. Churchill.

Lieutenant Winant was missing after a Flying Fortress daylight raid on Munster early in October last year.

Lord Haig and Lord Hopetoun have also been released, says Associated Press.

Others Freed

Princess Anne of France, 39-year-old widow of the Duke of Aosta, former Italian Viceroy of Abyssinia, arrived in Switzerland yesterday from Bavaria, where French troops released her. She was accompanied by the children of her sister-in-law, Princess Irene of Greece, Duchess of Aosta.

Others freed include M. Daladier Prime Minister when France declared war, and Reynaud, Prime Minister at the time of the French collapse, General Gamelin, French Commander-in-Chief at the outbreak of war, and General Weygand, who took over when the Germans broke though on the Meuse.

Leon Blum, former socialist Prime Minister of France, was hurried away a few hours before the camp was captured, said a S.H.A.E.F. statement last night. But a late message from Reuter, said Schussning, former Austrian Premier: Admiral Horthy, former Hungarian Regent: Pastor Niemoller: and the former French Premier, Leon Blum, were yesterday discovered to be in Northern Italy.

Jean Borotra, the Basque tennis star, has also been liberated.

The article not only shows how well thought of Lascelles actually was by the people of the village of Harewood, who appeared genuinely happy on hearing the news that he was safe and would shortly be on his way home, but also that the un-named reporter who compiled the article appeared to be under the impression that the Germans simply handed the Viscount, and all those who were being held with him, over to the US 7th Army at the cessation of hostilities, which of course, was not the case. There was absolutely no mention whatsoever of German and American soldiers fighting side by side at Itter Castle, against elements of the SS to save those being held there. Neither was there any mention of the somewhat salubrious conditions Lascelles and those with him, were being held in. The article made it sound like they had been detained in a standard style POW camp.

After having been released from his captivity, Viscount Lascelles returned to England and his ancestorial home, Harewood House, in West Yorkshire, which had been built in the eighteenth century, for Edwin Lascelles, 1st Baron Harewood.

The *Daily Mirror* newspaper, dated Monday, 7 May 1945, included the following article about the attack at Itter:

Members of the German garrison of the tiny medieval castle at Itter, near Innsbruck, in the

Austrian Tyrol, fought alongside Americans when 300 S.S. men attacked the castle after its surrender.

Prisoners in the castle included fifteen well known French men and women, among them Daladier and Reynaud, the French ex-Premiers, General Gamelin, Jean Borotra the tennis star, and the sister of General de Gaulle.

A cable from DAVID WALKER says that these prisoners were among the many well-known captives the Germans planned to hold as hostages in a vast Nazi bargaining scheme.

They were guarded by forty members of the Wehrmacht and the German Major in command, hearing that the Americans were near, went out to give in to them.

He escorted a tank back to the castle with a party of U.S. soldiers, when the S.S. men in the surrounding woods, hearing of the surrender opened fire, obviously determined that their hostages should not be lost.

A hail of 88mm shells landed all around the castle.

Immediately and without question the Wehrmacht garrison joined with the tiny American force to fight back the attackers with every weapon at their disposal.

During the battle, Borotra slipped out, crawled through the woods, and managed to contact the Americans in the neighbouring small town of Wörgl.

He led a column of infantry and the 12th U.S. Armored Division back to the castle where, after a sharp engagement, the attacking Germans were pounded into surrender.

The German Major, who had fought so well alongside the Americans, was among the small number of casualties.

Despite the news for these articles no doubt originating from the same source, this article from a national newspaper was a lot smaller and contained much less detail, although it does mention that American and German forces fought alongside each other against the attacking SS force.

The *Daily News* (London) newspaper dated Monday, 7 May 1945, included the following article about the battle:

There was a fierce four-hour battle in and around the castle before M. Daladier and other prominent Frenchmen were liberated after two years' incarceration.

German troops fought alongside the Americans of the 36th Division against their fellow countrymen after a German Major had come out and offered to surrender the castle.

Among the personalities freed from this secret prison by the US Seventh Army were:

M. Daladier, who was the French Premier of France when the war broke out, resigned in

March 1940, and became Minister of Defence in M. Reynaud's Cabinet.

M. Reynaud, who resigned in June of that year to give way to Marshal Petain's Cabinet.

General Gamelin, C-in-C of the French land troops at the outbreak of the war, appointed C-in-C of the Allied forces shortly afterwards, superseded by Gen. Weygand.

General Weygand, French C-in-C in May 1940, became Defence Minister in Marshal Petain's Cabinet in June of that year, and was given the task of assuring the defence of the French Empire.

Dr. Schuschnigg, former Chancellor of Austria, and M. Leon Blum, former Socialist Premier of France, had been imprisoned there, but were hurried away a few hours before the castle was captured.

To a Third Army Command Post there arrived under Swiss diplomatic protection: Viscount Lascelles, son of the Princess Royal; Captain John Elphinstone, a nephew of the Queen; Gen Bor-Komorowski, who led the rising of Polish patriots in Warsaw in August 1944; Lt. John Winant, son of the US Ambassador in Britain; Lt. Felix de Hamel, a relative of Mr Churchill; and Lt. Michael Alexander, a cousin of Field-Marshal Alexander.

The French First Army freed Gen. de Gaulle's sister-in-law, and the son of Georges Clemenceau, Frances's last war victory Premier.

A further news story from Monday, 7 May 1945 covered the event in a different way from the previous articles. The *Belfast Telegraph* newspaper dated Tuesday, 8 May 1945 (the day after the event), included the following article written by their correspondent, Evelyn Irons:

> In a lakeside hotel I took part in a historic reunion. The return to the French lines of notable Frenchmen freed by Americans from the Tyrolean castle of Itter, where they were imprisoned by the Nazis.
>
> General De Lattre de Tassigny was there to welcome them. The party included Reynaud, Daladier, Generals Weygand and Gamelin, Trade union leader Jouhaux, Mme. Cailliau (General de Gaulle's sister) and her husband, tennis champion Jean Borotra.
>
> Commandant William Bullitt, former American Ambassador in Paris, who is now on General de Lattres de Tassigny's Staff, greeted Daladier enthusiastically. Daladier kept himself fit in internment by playing deck tennis with Borotra, who gave him an owe-30 handicap and various other advantages.
>
> I had a long talk with spruce haired Reynaud, who said, 'France will continue to fight alongside the Allies in the Pacific War. It is most important to keep up the strongest Franco-British amity.'

He told me he had read and written much during his five years in prison. He had 300 books sent to him and spent most of his time in study.

'I don't think prison does a man such a lot of harm,' he said, 'I find plenty of opportunity for work and thought.'

It is interesting that reports about what took place at Itter Castle, and other similar locations, and the details of the individuals who had been held there, made it into the Press so quickly. From a British perspective, it is unclear as to whether King George VI and Queen Elizabeth, along with Prime Minister Winston Churchill, knew where their relatives were being held, or even if they knew whether they were alive or dead. If those held at the castle were allowed to write letters home to loved ones, they most definitely would not have been allowed to include the location of where they were being held.

The *Belfast Newsletter*, dated Tuesday, 8 May 1945, included a small article on the bottom of page two, squeezed in between the greyhound and horse racing results from the previous day. It was about two of the British prisoners who had been held at Itter Castle, and who had now returned home:

Welcomed at Palace

Lieutenant Viscount Lascelles, nephew of the King, and Captain the Master of Elphinstone, the nephew of the Queen, were welcomed at Buckingham Palace last night by the King and Queen and Princess Elizabeth. Both were among special "hostage" prisoners of war who had been liberated.

A number of photographs appeared in *The Sphere* newspaper dated Saturday, 19 May 1945. Page twenty-six of that day's edition included eight images reportedly about the liberation of prisoners who had reportedly been held captive at Itter Castle in Austria. One of the images was of five men leaning against an official looking car. These were Lieutenant De Hamel, Lieutenant Viscount Lascelles; Captain the Master of Elphinstone; Lieutenant Alexander; and Werner Buchmuller, an attaché of the Swiss Red Cross organization.

Excluding Buchmuller, all the men are in military uniform, although Viscount Lascelles is seen wearing a non-military issue white and blue striped shirt under his battledress top, as it was the only one he had left.

The men all look fit and in good health, suggesting the conditions in which they had been held had not been too much of a hardship. They had clearly been reasonably well looked after and well fed during their period of incarceration. For each of them, the war was finally over.

CHAPTER ELEVEN

Operation *Cowboy* – 28 April 1945

The only other occasion during the Second World War when American and German Wehrmacht soldiers fought side by side against forces of the Waffen-SS was in the German-occupied Czechoslovakian village of Hostau (now Hostouň, Czech Republic), on 28 April 1945, just a week before the equally remarkable events which took place at Itter Castle.

In many respects, this battle was even more incredible because the fighting there did not concern VIPs detained by the Nazis to use at a later time as potential hostages, but more than 300 Lipizzaner horses of the Academy of Classical Horsemanship, better known as the Spanish Riding School, which had been relocated from Vienna to a large farm in Hostau before the war had begun. Just as the Nazi wished breed a superior Aryan race, it would seem they also wanted to do the same with horses.

The man in charge of the riding school was Alois Podhajsky, a Major in the German Wehrmacht, who as a younger man before the war had been a Colonel in the Austrian Army. He had competed in the dressage events of the 1936 Berlin Olympics, where he had won a bronze medal, and would later do the same in the first post-war Olympics held in London in 1948.

The Yalta Conference between the British Prime Minister Winston Churchill, the Soviet leader, Josef Stalin, and the American President Franklin D. Roosevelt, had taken place in February 1945. The main topic of the conference was to discuss and determine the post-war state of Germany and Europe, and to decide which parts of the continent would come under the control of each the victorious Allied nations. Hostau in Czechoslovakia was part of the area allocated to the forces of the Soviet Union.

For most of the war food had been scarce for both military personnel as well as civilians. As the war dragged on, food shortages became even more acute. To some the very idea of feeding horses instead of humans was wrong, especially as to some, hundreds of horses, which included the prized Lipizzaners, could provide an awful lot of steaks and burgers.

With large numbers of hungry and tired Soviet soldiers closing in from the east on their way to the Czechoslovakian capital of Prague, it was believed that although the horses were prized Lipizzaners, the Soviets would simply see them as much needed food and kill them all. These were genuine fears, as the Soviets had already proven their lack of concern or care towards the Royal Hungarian Lipizzaner collection by slaughtering large numbers of them, whilst those that were not killed were used as work horses.

The other issue involved the German Wehrmacht soldiers who were stationed at the farm, who were understandably more concerned about their own wellbeing than that of the horses they were there helping to protect. They would have been aware of the imminent arrival of both the American and Soviet forces and so the decision they had to make was whether to remain at their post and continue to protect the horses in their care, or whether they would try to escape towards the west where the XII Corps of the US Third Army were advancing from, just in case Soviet forces were the first to arrive at the farm.

Life on the Hostau farm was further complicated for the officers who were there because they also had their wives and children with them. But this luxury came at a price. As the war drew to a close and Soviet forces advanced towards the farm, the lives of the officers' families were in real danger, and they knew it only too well.

The two most senior officers at the farm were Lieutenant Colonel Hubert Rudofsky, who was in overall charge of the farm's military vets, and intelligence officer Walter Holters. Both men were in agreement that they had to do all they could to save as many of the farm's horses as possible, but in particular the Lipizzaners. To this end they sent one of their military vets, Hauptmann Dr Rudolf Lessing, a blonde-haired blue-eyed man, who earlier in the war had seen active service on the Eastern Front, to make contact with American forces.

Lessing, an officer and gentleman with film star looks, rode out of the school with two of the prized Lipizzaners and made his way as fast as he could towards the American lines. Fortunately for Lessing, when he reached the Bohemian Forest, the first American soldiers he bumped into were from the US 42nd Cavalry Reconnaissance Squadron of the 2nd Cavalry Group, who by then were no longer on horseback, as their name maybe suggested, but in trucks and tanks. Their commanding officer was Colonel Charles Hancock Reed, who prior to the war had been a horse breeder, and also happened to be a former cavalryman, as well as a big fan of equestrian eventing. A number of Reed's junior officers had previously served in mounted units prior to when their horses had been swapped for mechanised vehicles.

After Lessing had explained the situation regarding the horses to Reed, and despite the fact he and his men were about to make their way to Weissensulz, in Czechoslovakia, to rescue some Allied POWs, he directed a number of his men to make their way to Hostau to safeguard the horses and liberate the Allied POWs being held there. To be able to do this, Reed had to first obtain the agreement of General George Patton. With every soldier being a valuable and much-needed resource at such an important time of the war, convincing Patton of the importance of saving the horses was not a forgone conclusion by any stretch of the imagination, but Patton agreed, and the operation went ahead.

Reed clearly understood the importance of rescuing the horses, and by his actions potentially prevented the breed from becoming extinct, although history has tended to give the overall credit for this to General Patton.

Reed's 325 men, under the command of Major Robert P. Andrews, and travelling in a combination of M8 Scout Cars, M8 Howitzer Motor Carriages, and M24 Chaffee Light Tanks, arrived safely at the farm in Hostau to discover Allied POWs and a large number of horses, which included thoroughbreds and prized Arabians as well as the Lipizzaners. The 20-mile journey to the farm had not been without incident, after Wehrmacht soldiers at the German–Czechoslovakian border had to be deterred from challenging the American rescue convoy by the intervention of an artillery bombardment. Reaching Hostau had been the easier aspect of the operation, which in earnest only really began once the evacuation of the horses was underway.

Major Roberts quickly grasped the enormity of the situation he found himself in. One of the first things he realised was that to be able to safely evacuate all the horses and move them back behind American lines, he would require the assistance of more men than had arrived with him at the farm. Thinking on his feet, as any competent officer would be expected to do in such circumstances, he decided not only to utilise the Allied POWs he had just liberated, but also the farm's German Wehrmacht guards, who despite being prisoners of the

Americans, had absolutely no desire to run the risk of falling into the hands of the quickly advancing Soviet forces from the east. So dire was the situation, Roberts also took the unusual decision of handing the German POWs their weapons back.

Roberts had the added bonus of having the number of men at his disposal increased with the addition of about two dozen men of the 1st Cossack Cavalry Division from the XV SS Cavalry Corps, under the command of Prince Amassov, who had deserted. These soldiers had arrived at the farm, along with their families and horses, prior to Roberts' arrival. Like the German soldiers who had been stationed at the farm, the Cossacks did not want to fall into the hands of Soviet forces. They looked resplendent in their part German, part Cossack uniforms, sat astride their impressive looking black Anglo-Kabarda horses. These were proud men who had no loyalty to Moscow, having been oppressed for many years by Stalin and the Communist Party, and despite choosing to serve Hitler and the Nazi Party, they ended up having no love for them either.

For Lieutenant Colonel Hubert Rudofsky, having the assistance of the Cossacks was somewhat of a Catch-22 situation. On the one hand he was glad of the extra manpower, men who had a proven fighting reputation, but men, their families, as well as nearly 200 horses, who he now had to find room for and feed at the farm.

Life for the Germans who had found themselves working at the Hostau farm had been a favourable existence up until this point in the war. If it had not been for their military uniforms and what passed for discipline, many of them would have been hard pushed to have known there was a war taking place. But as the war drew to a close, the reality of what was happening suddenly started to become very real.

Of the 350 American soldiers who took part in the operation, two died in the efforts to rescue the horses. Sergeant Owen Sutton was initially wounded at the farm in Hostau, and died of his wounds at a US Army field hospital in Nuremberg just a few days later. Private First Class Raymond Manz, who was only 19 years of age, was killed in action whilst part of a unit trying to take out a German roadblock attempting to prevent the horses from being removed from the farm.

CHAPTER TWELVE

Austrian Resistance

This story would not be complete without looking into the part that the Austrian Resistance played in the Battle of Itter Castle. The man in charge of the local Wörgl group was Rupert Hagleitner, and by May 1945, his group had seen their numbers increase following the arrival of Wehrmacht Major Josef Gangl and about ten of his men, who after having disobeyed an order to leave the town, instead choose to remain behind and protect the civilian population from the roaming hordes of SS men who were in the area at the time. The Austrian Resistance had been in place before the outbreak of the Second World War and had come about as a direct result of the rise of fascism throughout Europe, and particular that of Nazi Germany. The feeling of Austrian nationalism was heightened even further after the Anschluss of 1938, which resulted in the occupation of Austria by German armed forces.

There had been rumblings of an Austro-German unification in existence for many years, with those who viewed it as a positive vision of the future, whilst others took the opposite opinion and were not so supportive of the idea. Possibly because the thinking was to form a new nation known as 'Greater Germany', with there being absolutely no mention of an 'Austria' at all.

Throughout the years of the Second World War, it has been estimated that more than 100,000 people became part of the Austrian Resistance. Membership of such organisations came at a price in no matter which occupied nation they were from. Betrayal by a so-called friend or colleague or being captured by the Gestapo or other Germany Army units, was only ever going to be a bad experience and would usually involve interrogation, torture and or death.

There was a noticeable change in attitude towards the idea of unification after Adolf Hitler and the Nazi Party came to power in 1933. There were those who believed there were attempts by pro-Nazis to try to undermine the Austrian government and in doing so, destabilise the country.

What history has recorded as the July Putsch took place in Austria between 25 and 30 July 1934, and was an attempt by Austrian Nazis to carry out a coup against the democratically elected Austrian government. A force of Austrian Nazis and members of the German SS attacked the nation's Chancellery building in Vienna, in an attempt at ousting the ruling Fatherland Front government led by Engelbert Dollfuss. The plan was to then replace Dollfuss with the leader of the Christian Social Party, the pro-Nazi Anton Rintelen. The attempted coup ultimately failed because both the Austrian people and the army stayed loyal to the government of Dollfuss, despite the fact he was killed during the attempted coup. His replacement, Kurt Schuschnigg, retained the support which Dollfuss had received, and the government of the Fatherland Front remained in power.

If the putsch had been successful, it is more than likely a German invasion of Austria would have taken place soon after.

Four years later, the Austrian Chancellor Kurt Schuschnigg announced that the nation's people would have the right to vote on the possibility of a union with Germany, or to maintain Austria's independence and sovereignty. The referendum was due to take place on 13 March 1938. Adolf Hitler was not impressed, claiming instead that most Austrians and Germans wanted the two nations to unite. On 12 March, the day before the proposed referendum, German forces crossed unopposed into Austria.

A Nazi-organised referendum took place in both Austria and Germany on 10 April 1938. After the voting had been completed, in what had been a near 100 percent turnout, it was announced that 99.73 percent of the votes were in favour of the two nations uniting as one.

Such occasions resulted in an increase in the numbers of Austrian citizens joining the resistance movement.

Despite the desire to fight against the evil tyranny of Nazism in their midst, when it came to the Battle of Itter Castle, it would be fair to say that the Austrian

Resistance was found to be somewhat lacking. Before the SS began their attack, Major Gangl contacted the resistance movement in Wörgl by telephoning the local leader, Rupert Hagleitner, and explaining the situation. Gangl's request for assistance did not fall on deaf ears and Hagleitner quickly sent reinforcements to the castle to help in its defence against the SS attack. This came in the form of just two Wehrmacht soldiers who had 'defected' to the Austrian Resistance, along with an Austrian youth.

With the war almost at an end, and the Tyrol region of Austria fast becoming the final bastion of the Nazis' Third Reich, all the Austrian Resistance movement in Wörgl could manage to muster were just three men, none of whom were hardened resistance fighters.

The answer to the earlier point about why there were not more resistance fighters sent to help protect the French dignitaries at Itter Castle might be more understandable if we take a look at the makeup of the Austrian Resistance movement, which could be described as somewhat splintered in its structure. As would be expected in a time of war, the strength of a resistance movement came from the number of separate and self-autonomous groups it was made from. If the resistance movement was simply one large organisation, it could be easily dismantled once its veil of secrecy had been penetrated and its leadership eradicated.

The Austrian Resistance was made up of both non-partisan as well as armed groups, many of which were quite diverse. A number of them were either run by members of the clergy or included men of the cloth. There were several communist or socialist-run groups, as well as those made up of Austrian civil servants, Austrians in exile, and those known as the 'Silent Heroes', with individuals drawn from the arts and academia.

Many of the activities conducted by the resistance movement were non-violent, focusing on such routine matters as producing anti-Nazi wartime political leaflets. They collected monies from members of the public, which was then split amongst families of those arrested and imprisoned by the Nazis. They also gathered military intelligence on German troop and unit movements throughout the county, which they then passed on to the Allies.

Armed resistance was a contradiction in terms as it certainly did not mean that they took the Germans on in direct armed combat. Most of this type of resistance involved the sabotage of, or attacks on, military installations such as barracks, or civilian targets such as railway lines.

One of the unanswered questions about the Battle of Itter Castle has always been why Josef Gangl decided to join the Austrian Resistance so late on in the war, especially as before then he had fought for his country against the Allies in such a passionate and brave manner, even being awarded the Iron Cross 2nd and 1st Class for his actions. The answer to this question might possibly be found in a visit that Gangl is said to have made to the main Dachau concentration camp, where the shock of what he saw and witnessed was such that he felt he had no other option but to join the resistance movement to help prevent the murder of any more innocent civilians by elements of the SS, and who for the most part were loyal and dedicated members of the Nazi Party.

A list of known members of the Austrian Resistance from Wörgl and the surrounding areas is included in Appendix A.

CHAPTER THIRTEEN

After the Battle

Thanks to the presence of the French-Canadian war correspondent and journalist, René Lévesque, the Jewish American war correspondent Meyer Levin, and French military photographer Éric Schwab, the Battle of Itter Castle was quickly and accurately reported. Were this not the case, it may well have been some years after the war before the incident came to light, by which time it would have become just another footnote of the war.

Although a number of the defenders were wounded or injured during the battle, it is remarkable that only one person was killed; the German Wehrmacht officer, Major Josef Gangl. Despite his military status, he was buried in Wörgl's main cemetery, not because of his efforts at Itter Castle, but for deciding to stay behind when ordered to leave so as to help protect the town's civilian population from marauding members of the SS, who were intent on killing anybody they perceived had committed the smallest of misdemeanours.

Regardless of the actual reason behind Gangl's actions at Itter Castle, it is abundantly clear what the population of Wörgl thought about him, even renaming a street in their town after him. He was also seen as a hero by the surviving members of the Austrian Resistance movement, who unveiled a small memorial honouring his name in the town, stating that he 'died a hero's death'.

Very soon after the battle, the castle's liberated French dignitaries were quickly returned to France, which for tennis star Jean Borotra initially resulted in his arrest by French authorities for what was seen by them as his 'collaboration' with the Vichy government, although he was never subsequently charged with having committed any offences. His involvement in tennis continued until shortly before his death in 1994 when he was 95 years of age.

It is pure guess work as to what the knock-on effect would have been if the castle had been breached and overrun by the SS, and the French dignitaries inside had been murdered. Two of them, Reynaud and Daladier, subsequently held high political positions in future French governments. Paul Reynaud was elected to the Chamber of Deputies in 1946, and also held several cabinet positions in the French government. Christiane Mabire, who had been with him during his stay at Itter Castle, and had previously been held at Ravensbrück concentration camp, became his wife in 1949. The couple went on to have three children, who of course would have never been born if the couple had been murdered by the SS.

Édouard Daladier was re-elected as a member of the Chamber of Deputies, also in 1946; a position he went on to hold until 8 December 1958. He had previously been a member of the same body between 16 November 1919 and 10 July 1940. In 1953 he also became the Mayor of Avignon.

A few of the French dignitaries held at Itter Castle went on to write their memoires, which not surprisingly included their version of the events which saw American and German troops fight alongside each other against elements of the SS.

As for Lieutenant John Carey 'Jack' Lee, his actions and leadership on 4 and 5 May at Itter Castle subsequently saw him awarded the United States Distinguished Service Cross, the citation of which was included in General Orders No. 212, issued by the Headquarters section of US Forces, European Theater of War, and read as follows:

> For extraordinary heroism in connection with military operations against an enemy while serving with Company B, 23rd Tank Battalion, in action against enemy forces on 4 and 5 May 1945. Captain Lee's intrepid actions, personal bravery and zealous devotion to duty exemplify the highest traditions of the military forces of the United States and reflect great credit upon himself, his unit, and the United States Army.

His brothers, William and David, also served their country during the course of the war as privates in the

United States Army. David was awarded the Bronze Star and the Purple Heart for his wartime service.

Lee left the army on 27 April 1946 and settled back into civilian life, but it was ten years before he met and married Dorothy J. Dagnell on 1 May 1956 in Orange, California, by which time Lee was 38 and his new bride some thirteen years younger at 25.

Despite the award of the Distinguished Service Cross, which will forever connect him to the events that took place at Itter Castle on 4/5 May 1945, Lee's life once he returned home after the war was nothing out of the ordinary, and certainly not as might have been expected of such a man.

There is no comprehensive road map of Lee's post-war life, but it would be fair to say that like many of his compatriots who returned home after the war, there were no guarantees of a better life, wealth, and happiness, in fact for many of them, including Lee, there was just the normal trials and tribulations of everyday life. Without the events that took place at Itter Castle in the early days of May 1945, the Second World War would have more than likely passed by without Lee's name ever being mentioned, other than possibly in relation to his unit's annual re-union dinners. He certainly would not have received a bravery award.

Lee passed away on 15 January 1973, at the relatively young age of 54, in his hometown of Norwich and was buried at Saint Paul's Cemetery, Norwich, Chenango County, New York.

SS officer Kurt Schrader, who had assisted in the defence of the castle when asked to do so by the French prisoners held there, was arrested at the end of the war, not because he had committed any specific war crimes, but because he was a member of the SS, which had been designated a 'proscribed organisation' by the Allied authorities. Despite not being charged with any wartime related offences, he was still incarcerated for two years before eventually being released in 1947.

On his release from captivity, Schrader somehow managed to acquire a position working in the Interior Ministry of the region of North Rhine-Westphalia in what became West Germany. This was an unusual appointment as the Allies did not usually like the idea of former members of the SS being put into such high positions of government, either at a local or national level, because of concerns of the potential political influence they might end up exercising. Maybe it was because of the help he provided to the French prisoners, and the fight against the SS, that his position within the region's Interior Ministry so readily came about.

During the war he was awarded the *Verwundetenabzeichen*, or wound badge, which was awarded to members of the Wehrmacht, SS, and the auxiliary service organizations. He was also awarded the *Winterschlacht Im Osten*, or the Eastern Front Medal, which was first awarded on 26 May 1942, for those men who had served on the Eastern Front between 15 November 1941 and 15 April 1942. Schrader was also a recipient of the *Eisernes Kreuz*, of the Iron Cross, had first been awarded in 1813 during the time of the Napoleonic wars. Although purely a military award, there were occasions when it was also awarded to civilians who had carried out military actions.

Conclusion

What happened at Itter Castle is a tale about the victory of good over the tyranny of evil. It shows the good in mankind whilst at the same time also showing the evil intent it was possible for others to display.

It recounts the heroism and bravery displayed by several individuals, including such men as Lieutenant Jack Lee, Jean Borotra, Zvonimir Čučković, Andreas Krobot, Kurt Schrader, and Major Josef Gangl. Each of them displayed personal bravery and heroism in assisting a group of individuals most of them had never met and knew absolutely nothing about.

Lee's part in it is simple and straight forward. He was a soldier simply doing his job, fighting enemy combatants in an effort to protect civilian lives. Čučković had been a Croatian communist resistance fighter before he had been captured and had no great love of the Germans, especially members of the SS. By offering to go for help, he was simply utilising his innate skills. Borotra, a famous tennis player, had served in the French Army during the First World War and had been a member of the French Vichy government in the early years of the war. Krobot, although the castle's cook, had a feeling of self-preservation and a natural desire to stay alive.

As for Schrader and Gangl, their reasons for taking the actions they did are not so clear. Schrader was, after all, an officer in the SS, so it is especially hard to understand from his perspective not so much why he would have assisted those held captive at Itter Castle, but why he would have so easily considered turning against his comrades. It is also known that he sought written confirmation from the French dignitaries in connection to the assistance he had provided to them. Why did he feel the need to make such a request unless he knew that in the immediate aftermath of the war he might just require such documentation? The suggestion is that he did not help those in the castle out of the kindness of his heart, but more out of self-preservation because he had realised that the war was fast coming to an end and that Germany were going to be the losers.

In the case of Josef Gangl, it is even more difficult to understand his actions at Itter Castle, by which time he had served in the German Army for fifteen years. A seasoned soldier in every sense of the word. If he had a dislike of Adolf Hitler and the Nazi Party, he had never previously publicly voiced his views or concerns. His actions in the build up to and during the battle are commendable and ultimately his bravery cost him his life. But, as in the case of Schrader, the question has to be asked, why the sudden change of heart? His conscience only appears to have been pricked after the reported death of Adolf Hitler, and a matter of days before German leaders signed an unconditional surrender to finally bring the Second World War to an end. Here was a highly decorated individual who had served his country bravely and honourably, but it has to be said, this was something he did willingly.

In April 1945, during the latter stages of the war, an estimated 1.5 million German and Axis forces were captured on the Western Front. Most of the Nazi concentration camps had been liberated by the end of April 1945.

All German forces withdrew from Finland on 25 April 1945, and Hitler committed suicide on the 30th.

On 2 May, nearly 1 million German forces in Italy and Austria surrendered unconditionally to British Field Marshal Sir Harold Alexander. The same day Berlin fell, when General Helmuth Weidling surrendered the city to Soviet General, Vasily Chuikov.

On 4 May, German forces in north-west Germany, Denmark, and the Netherlands surrendered. The same day British Field Marshal Bernard Montgomery took the unconditional surrender at Lüneburg from Generaladmiral Hans-Georg von Friedeburg, and General Eberhard Kinzel of all German forces in Holland, in north-west Germany including the Frisian Islands, Heligoland and all other islands, Schleswig-Holstein, and Denmark. The number of German land, sea and air forces involved in this surrender amounted to 1 million men.

On 5 May, Großadmiral (Admiral of the Fleet) Dönitz ordered all U-boats to cease offensive operations and return to their bases. Later the same day, Generaloberst (Colonel General) Johannes Blaskowitz surrendered to Canadian Commander Lieutenant General Charles Foulkes in the Dutch town of Wageningen, in the presence of Prince Bernhard of the Netherlands, the acting Commander-in-Chief of the Dutch Interior Forces.

On 5 May 1945, German forces in Bavaria surrendered when General Hermann Foertsch stood down all German forces stationed between the Bohemian mountains and the Upper Inn River to American General Jacob L. Devers, commanding officer of the American 6th Army Group.

So, despite it being blatantly clear that the war was clearly coming to an end, and that Germany and her allies would be the vanquished, a diehard group of young SS men were not only intent on continuing the fight, but they wanted to murder a group of aging French civilians who were inside Itter Castle, being protected by a small group of young German Wehrmacht soldiers who were stood shoulder to shoulder alongside their American counterparts.

On 6 May, Generaloberst Jodl and Generalfeld-marschall Keitel surrendered all German armed forces unconditionally. Jodl arrived in Reims and offered to surrender all forces fighting the Allies. The Supreme Allied Commander, General Dwight D. Eisenhower, informed Jodl that he would only accept a complete and unconditional surrender of all German forces. Eisenhower also informed Jodl that if he refused to accept those terms, he would force all German forces who were

still fighting to surrender to the Soviets. After first contacting Admiral Dönitz, who was in Flensburg, informing him of Eisenhower's declaration, Dönitz, accepting
the inevitable, agreed to the complete and total surrender of all German forces. For some of those who had
taken part in the Battle of Itter Castle, this agreement
came too late.

List of known Wörgl Resistance Fighters

(Names in bold known to have taken part in the Battle of Itter Castle)

Berger, Thomas
Blattl, Lorenz
Böheim, Franz
Buratti, Rochus
Coleselli, Engelbert
Damm, Fritz
Foidl, Josef
Gasperi, Johann
Grimm, Erwin
Hable, Rudolf
Hagleitner, Rupert
Hauser, Balthasar
Hauser, Hermann
Hechenberger, Josef

Langhofer, Georg
Leitner, Pepi
Lenk, Andreas
Mayr, Alois
Mayrhofer, Sepp
Neumaier, Leo
Obrist, Anton
Pichler, Martin
Seißl, Andra
Seißl, Josef
Seißl, Leonhard
Sössi, Anton
Speigl, Hermann
Waltl, Hans

Wieser, Franz

Wilhelm, Anton

Winder, Georg

Zak, Heinrich

Zangerl, Josef

Zangerl Jnr, Josef

Individuals and Dignitaries Held at Itter Castle

Jean Robert Borotra – French tennis player and former member of Vichy Government.

Madame Janine Borotra – Wife of Jean Borotra.

Michel Clemenceau – Son of former Prime Minister of France.

Édouard Daladier – Former Prime Minister of France.

Marie-Agnes Cailliau – Sister of French General Charles de Gaulle.

Alfred Cailliau – Husband of Marie-Agnes Cailliau.

Maurice Gamelin – General & former Commander-in-Chief French Armed Forces.

Léon Jouhaux – Trade Union Leader.

Augustine Brüchlen – Secretary and mistress of Léon Jouhaux.

François de La Rocque – Right Wing Politician.

Albert François Lebrun – Former President of France.

André François-Poncet – Politician and Diplomat.

Paul Reynaud – Former Prime Minister of France.

Christiane Mabire – Long term mistress and later wife of Paul Reynaud.

Maxime Weygand – Former Chief of Staff of the French Army.

Madame Marie-Renée Weygand – Wife of Maxime Weygand.

General Tadeusz Bor-Komorowski – Commander-in-Chief Polish Military Forces.

General Tadeusz Pełczyński – General Komorowski's Deputy.

Sources

www.historyhub.history.gov

www.worldcat.org

www.praguepost.com

www.militaryhistorynow.com

www.warfarehistorynetwork.com

www.encyclopedia.ushmm.org

www.correspondent.afp.com

www.nationalinterest.org

www.tracesofwar.com

www.britannia.com

www.12tharmoredmuseum.com

www.historynet.com

www.stormfront.org

www.historyofthewaffenss.com

www.doew.at

A History of the U S Army 12th Armored Division, 15
     September 1942 - 17 December 1945
The T-Patch News, Tuesday 8 May 1945
The Hellcat News, Saturday 26 May 1945
The Neue Berliner Illustrierte, 5 September 1946
The National Archives of the United States
British Newspaper Archive
Wörgl City Archive
Clarissa Schnabel

Author Biography

Stephen is a happily retired police officer having served with Essex Police as a constable for thirty years between 1983 and 2013. He is married to Tanya, who is also his best friend.

Both his sons, Luke and Ross, were members of the armed forces, collectively serving five tours of Afghanistan between 2008 and 2013. Both were injured on their first tour. This led to Stephen's first book *Two Sons in a Warzone – Afghanistan: The True Story of a Fathers Conflict*, which was published in October 2010.

Both of Stephen's grandfathers served in and survived the First World War, one with the Royal Irish Rifles, the other in the Mercantile Navy, whilst his father was a member of the Royal Army Ordinance Corp during and after the Second World War.

Stephen corroborated with one of his writing partners, Ken Porter, on a previous book published in August 2012, *German POW Camp 266 – Langdon Hills*. They have also collaborated on four books in the 'Towns & Cities in the Great War' series by Pen and Sword.

Stephen has co-written three crime thrillers which were published between 2010 and 2012, and centre round a fictional detective named Terry Danvers.

When he is not writing, Stephen and Tanya enjoy the simplicity of going out for a morning coffee, lunch time meals or walking their four German shepherd dogs early each morning, whilst most sensible people are still fast asleep in their beds.

Other works for Pen & Sword include:

The Surrender of Singapore: Three Years of Hell 1942-45 (2017)
Against All Odds: Walter Tull, The Black Lieutenant. (2018)
Animals in the Great War (2018) (co-written with Tanya Wynn) *A History of the Royal Hospital Chelsea – 1682-2017: The Warriors Repose.* (co-written with Tanya Wynn) (2019)
Disaster before D-Day: Unravelling the Tragedy of Slapton Sands (2019)
Mystery of Missing Flight F-BELV (2020)
City of London at War: 1938 - 45 (2020)
Holocaust: The Nazis' Wartime Jewish Atrocities (2020)
Churchill's Flawed Decisions: Errors in Office of the Greatest Britain (2020)
The Lancastria Tragedy: Sinking and Cover-up 1940 (2020)
The Rise & Fall of Imperial Japan (2020)
The Shetland 'Bus': Transporting Secret Agents Across The North Sea (2021)
Dunkirk and the Aftermath (2021)
St Nazaire Raid, 1942 (2022)
The Blackout Ripper: A Serial Killer in London, 1942 (2022)
HMS Turbulent (2023)
Dieppe 1942 (2023)

Index